D0563714

YOU CAN
Get Over
Divorce

A 7-STEP GUIDE
TO SPEED THE HEALING
AND GET ON WITH
THE REST OF YOUR LIFE

Pat Hudson, Ph.D.

Prima Publishing

© 1998 by Pat Hudson

All rights reserved. No part of this book may be reproduced or transmitted in any form or by any means, electronic or mechanical, including photocopying, recording, or by any information storage or retrieval system, without written permission from Prima Publishing, except for the inclusion of quotations in a review.

PRIMA PUBLISHING and colophon are registered trademarks of Prima Communications, Inc.

Library of Congress Cataloging-in-Publication Data

Hudson, Patricia Olwen.
    You can get over divorce : a 7-step guide to speed the healing and get on with the rest of your life / by Pat Hudson.
        p. cm.
    Includes index.
    ISBN 0-7615-1608-5
    1. Divorce. 2. Divorce—Psychological aspects. I. Title.
HQ814.H777   1998
306.89—dc21   98-8582
                                                                    CIP

98 99 00 01 HH 10 9 8 7 6 5 4 3 2 1
Printed in the United States of America

Pseudonyms are used throughout to protect the privacy of the individuals involved.

How to Order
Single copies may be ordered from Prima Publishing, P.O. Box 1260BK, Rocklin, CA 95677; telephone (916) 632-4400. Quantity discounts are also available. On your letterhead, include information concerning the intended use of the books and the number of books you wish to purchase.

Visit us online at www.primapublishing.com

To my father,
R. Lofton Hudson—
Eighty-nine and still an inspiration.

CONTENTS

Contents

ACKNOWLEDGMENTS

THIS BOOK and all the learning that went into it are the sum of many parts that were contributed to me throughout my life. Parents, teachers, clients, friends, other writers, and even enemies all donated the elements of construction that built the ideas within these pages.

A particularly devoted group of friends, including my writers' group, were kind enough to read early drafts of the book and give me much-needed feedback. Specifically Toni Lombardi, Jody Sacone, Nina Atwood, Diane England, Rachel Williams, Rebekah Rosenthal, and Johnny Wise all donated their time to perfecting the manuscript—they are all on my gratitude list.

A special thanks always goes to my daughter, Angela Hexum, who understands the writer's life and mine so well, and who gives me that extra shove when needed.

My father, who now has 22 published books, is the beacon of influencing others' lives through writing that lights my way.

In the business of making things happen, my agent Jim Levine has stood by me in some of the rough times of my writing career. The folks at Prima have made getting the book out easy—Michelle McCormack, Julia Mc-Donald, and Elizabeth Haydu—I feel lucky to have had their timely support in birthing the book.

I have been truly blessed to have my path crossed by the people mentioned here.

INTRODUCTION

Experience is not what happens to a man; it is what a man does with what happens.

—ALDOUS HUXLEY

IN 1993 a friend of mine called me on the telephone. She had an edge of panic in her voice. "Pat, I just came from a lecture on divorce where they said it could take me seven years to get over my marriage ending! You know I just filed. Does that mean that I won't be okay until the next century?"

When you go through a divorce, it is hard to imagine that you will ever be happy again, particularly when you read the discouraging predictions about how long it will be before you feel better. As a marriage counselor since 1975, and a talk-show host for five years, I have had a lot of experience helping people find ways to heal. Not only have I helped others, but I have also had to help myself.

When my first marriage ended, announcing that I was getting a divorce felt comparable to announcing that I had just been infected with the Ebola virus. No one in my family had ever divorced. I had married my first husband when I was barely 21 years old. What did I know about what I was going to need for life—or, for that matter, whom I would turn out to be?

In time, however, I was able to deal with the shame and grief and began to look forward to finding a mate who would give me the marriage I wanted. I then married a fellow therapist, earnestly believing that I had made a match for life. So when my second husband moved out 10 years later, I was stunned, angry, and devastated. Public embarrassment was heaped on top of the pain. Because we had written two books on marriage together, our divorce was carried in many newspapers throughout the country and was mentioned as a "tsk-tsk" on *Paul Harvey*, a nationally syndicated radio show. I desperately wanted relief from what I was feeling, and dreaded the years of grieving I thought could be ahead of me.

I'm a book addict, so I turned to the self-help section of the nearest bookstore. In all my searching, I found only books predicting what the divorcing person would experience. Although it was good to know that I wasn't the only one feeling crazy as I went through a divorce, I wanted something that would help me speed the healing process. No luck. When I can't find a book I need, I write it myself. I wanted a good book on self-hypnosis for my clients. Couldn't find it. Wrote my first book. I wanted books about women's issues and relationships that were chock full of practical ideas. Couldn't find them. Wrote the next three books. Here we are again. Book-shopping frustration has spawned another book with lots of how-to's for speeding your divorce recovery.

Introduction

I don't want to imply that the books telling you what you will go through are not useful. It is valuable to know that you are not going crazy, and that others are on a terrible emotional roller coaster too. But I don't want to see you stuck there. You are going to grieve. You can't avoid it altogether, unless you never loved or cared about your spouse. It is natural to be sad about the loss, even if you initiated the divorce. You still are letting go of the dreams and optimism you had when you fell in love and got married.

There are many residual losses in divorce: your former in-laws, perhaps the house you had together, time with your children, and possibly financial security. You may miss being a family, even if you do not miss your former mate. The changes are often hard to imagine before you actually start living the divorced life. Be ready for that, but don't get stuck in your anger and grief. That is what this book is about—moving on from all those losses and resentments.

If you picked up this book thinking, "Maybe I should consider divorce," let me encourage you to work on your marriage. Having been through this twice, I can tell you it is rarely worth the hell you go through on the chance that you might be happier with someone else. Having another party lined up waiting for you to exit your marriage does not usually work. Starting a second marriage on the footing of having deceived someone else or giving up too easily creates an atmosphere of distrust that may eventually infect the next marriage. My first husband and I separated with the intention to divorce, and then reconciled to work on the marriage even harder for another couple of years. Even though we did not stay together, I think we have had a relatively civilized divorce because we each feel that the other tried. As long as you or your children are not in danger, err on the side of trying too hard rather than giving up too quickly.

You may have picked up this book to help you get over a long-term relationship that was not marriage. When you have been with someone for years, the breakup is like a divorce. The principles in this book apply to marriages, long-term romances, or same-sex relationships. All these require healing efforts.

What does healing from divorce mean? It means that you are able to put any strong feelings about your spouse to rest. Any extreme emotions will slow down your healing. My father was a very skilled and learned psychotherapist—the author of 22 books. On the first Christmas after my divorce in 1982, I found myself feeling very sad for my ex. I said, "Dad, I feel so bad about his facing the holiday without us. He said he was dreading it because Christmas is such a family time." My father looked me straight in the eye and replied, "Who the hell made you his mother?!" I took this gruff advice to mean that I needed neither to rescue nor reform my ex. And neither do you.

The most common feelings during divorce are loneliness, anxiety, anger, suspicion, and confusion. Everything in your life is turned upside down. Your daily routine is thrown up in the air to land who knows where. Your social ties are disrupted. You worry that your soon-to-be ex is going to take advantage of you in the settlement.

Your plans for your future come into question and you face life issues on your own (which may not be all bad). But whatever you are feeling and however you are getting through each day now, I will give you some new ideas to move the process along.

In the movie *Shadowlands*, C. S. Lewis asks his student, "Do you think we read so we will know we are not alone?" One of the reasons I write is to feel connected to others. This book is like a very long letter to a friend trying to get through a divorce. I hope that by reading the many stories of others people's journeys through divorce, you will know you are not alone.

SEVEN STEPS TO HEALING FROM DIVORCE

THE SEVEN principles in this book can change your life if you know how to apply them. It is not necessary to apply them in any order. I suggest you read the book through, return to the steps that appealed to you the most, and begin with those steps. The next seven chapters will show you how to make these principles come alive for you by giving you a step-by-step approach to change.

1. Tell Your Story

Admitting that your divorce is real and happening is often difficult, particularly the first time you have to say,

"I'm divorced." Nonetheless, the first step is to admit to yourself that you are divorced, develop some way of understanding what happened, and create a brief story that encapsulates the reason for divorce. This will ease your way in social situations when people inevitably ask, "What happened?" And developing your story will give you a good picture of your marriage and why it ended, increasing the likelihood that you will avoid repeating the same mistake or jumping from the frying pan into fire. Creating the story of your divorce will help give you closure and is good preventative medicine against a future divorce.

2. Heal Your Imagination

Psychologists have known for years how crucial imagination is to mental health. You can use imagery in three ways to get over your divorce:

(1) To react less to the past
(2) To feel comfortable and healing in the present
(3) To rehabilitate your future

If you can't imagine it, you can't do it. In order to create a future of success and happiness, you first have to be able to picture it in your mind. The longer you were married, the less likely it is that you had any alternative dreams that did not include your spouse. Rehabilitating your dreams of the future is an important step in healing from a divorce. Whatever you concentrate upon tends to expand. If you concentrate on your history, then its power over you expands. If you concentrate on a happy future, a positive future tends to expand and pull you forward. Enrich your imagination and keep your focus on the positive aspects of your life now.

3. Celebrate Divorce

Our culture does not offer a standard ceremony of passage for the end of a relationship. In the vast majority of the cases, the court experience is a matter of a few less-than-satisfying minutes. In this step you create rituals that honor the fact that the part of your life as a particular person's partner is over, and a new era as the author of your destiny begins. You will learn how to select symbols, plan a ritual, and incorporate new vows and celebrations. Because there are moments of passage in the divorce process—moving out, moving forth, the day the divorce is final, anniversaries—you will probably want to do many rituals in the process of healing from your divorce. You may be thinking that you would feel silly doing this, but I have found that the people who are hesitant are often the ones who get the most benefit from a ceremony.

4. The Great Escape

Escaping is a fine way to relieve the stress of divorce, as long as you know what you are doing. This step means learning healthy avoidance by deliberately taking vacations from your problem. Lose yourself in your work;

escape into movies, novels, or writing letters to your imagined future spouse; be creative with art or crafts; do fun things with friends . . . use your imagination. All of these activities are fine as long as you are not harming yourself or your children in the process. And remember, casual dating can be fun, but healthy escape does *not* include jumping into another marriage to try to escape the pain of divorce!

5. The Mental Tune-Up

Changing the way you think about your divorce is a great way to help yourself heal. When you see your own point of view as the barrier to healing, you can stand up to the negative power of the divorce. You can reprogram your mental computer so that your mind will not be stuck in negative thoughts. We'll look at four different approaches:

(1) Repeating a prayer or a mantra (to release my anger I used the prayer "Help me to forgive my ex-husband" whenever I would think of him)

(2) Using oppositional thinking (for example, "I'm not going to let this divorce push me around anymore")

(3) Focusing on the needs of others to keep yourself from attending your own pity party

(4) Using gainful thinking (what gains has the loss of the marriage brought you? For example, you might think, "Now I have new opportunities to travel because of this loss.")

6. Fake It 'Til You Make It

In Alcoholics Anonymous they use the phrase "Fake it 'til you make it." Pretending is a powerful tool. A myth of our society has been that you have to feel a certain way to act a certain way. People say, "I can't make myself feel happy," but you can create the likelihood that you will feel happy by doing happy things. Feelings follow actions. There are four ways to select actions that would indicate being healed from divorce:

(1) Know what you would do if this were no longer a problem
(2) Observe others who seem to be successful in adjusting to post-divorce life
(3) Remember what you did before marriage
(4) Read about overcoming loss. Do those things now that could be called getting-over-the-loss actions and see what happens to your attitude

7. Love, the Best Cure of All

Clients often say, "I am a loving person. What am I going to do with my love now?" You can go on being a loving person, but in a broader, more universal way. Love yourself first, and let that love overflow to others. Focus your love on those around you—particularly those who have had even greater losses—and discover all the joy there is in giving. In the earlier steps we focused on a great future. Here we want to be completely in the present, experiencing gratitude for all the positive things in our lives and giving love to those around us. Being an active part of the loving force in the world is recovery.

To heal means to become whole, and no part of you will be left out of the healing process. Because divorce is such a gigantic change, it requires all parts of you to get the momentum going in the right direction. All your resources need to be available. In the following pages you will learn how to use these steps, as well as your mind, actions, imagination, heart, and soul to heal. The right direction is one of confidence in your ability to manage yourself as a single person or a single parent, to get your needs met, to create a new single life, and to manage your responses to the disappointment of divorce. By the time you finish this book, you will feel that confidence.

CHAPTER ONE

Tell
Your Story

Life can only be understood backwards;
but it must be lived forwards.

—SØREN KIERKEGAARD

IVORCE CHANGES the course of your life. Understandably, you want to get over your divorce and get on with your life—and quickly. But when something this momentous occurs, you need to understand what happened before you can move on. To do so quickly, you'll need to have some idea about why your marriage ended. The best way I have found is to take some time to construct your story.

WHY DO I NEED A STORY?

OUR BRAINS insist on organizing all our experiences into our ongoing histories. It is simply impossible to have something as dramatic as a divorce happen to you and let it remain unexplained. Since this is an inevitable process, taking charge of the situation and working on your story is a great first step to moving on from your divorce.

Your Untold Story Can Make You Sick

One good reason to tell your story is that if you do not acknowledge what happened, it may make you sick. We have all heard anecdotes about people who couldn't face the loss of their marriage, widowhood, death of a child, or loss of a business, and who clearly became ill as a result of bottled-up emotions. I have heard many of these tales about the damage that can occur from not being able to create or share one's story, but the one that sticks with me is what happened to a client of mine, Rebecca.

Rebecca's second husband had a romantic involvement in the first year of their marriage, and she could not understand how this could happen—their relationship seemed so good. Rebecca was more than hurt, she was embarrassed. She felt she could not tell her parents or others what had happened, because this secret was just too awful. Soon after, she became ill, and was sick for two years. Deep inside, she felt this illness was radiating from her unspoken shame. She went from doctor to doctor trying to find out why she had chronic sinus infections, extreme fatigue, and aching joints, but none of the doctors could help her. Finally, after another one of her husband's affairs, she asked for a divorce. This time, she acknowledged her husband's infidelity and told her story. She said to herself as he left, "He made me sick once by betraying me. I am not going to let it happen again." Rebecca sailed through the divorce with no serious physical symptoms. Unlike before, she did not live in secret shame. She was certain that if she had somehow stuffed all the hurt and anger inside again, she would have become ill.

Sharing Your Life with Others

People are social creatures, and we usually share our histories with others. When people hear you are divorced, they will naturally want to know what happened. If you don't have a story about your divorce, you will either seem to lack insight about your life or appear secretive. Whether you are at a family reunion, a cocktail party, or on an airplane, you will need some way to tell people what happened without telling every intimate detail of your life. Here are some examples:

- "Our values were too different. It became too miserable for both of us."
- "When it came to intimacy, the gap between what he wanted and what I wanted was too great."
- "She just couldn't handle the burdens of adult married life, so she left the kids and me."
- "He had a midlife crisis and married a younger woman."
- "She had a drinking problem and refused treatment."

A longer story may be more accurate, but a short story is more appropriate for social occasions or casual acquaintances. You may find it uncomfortable to share your complete and true story with most people. In this case, opt for a public explanation that is close to the truth. For example, Liz's husband was a cross-dresser. Because he would insist on wearing a nightgown at night, Liz was unable to approach him sexually. She could no longer tolerate this problem, and asked for a divorce. For the sake of their two daughters, however, her summary was that they had "too many conflicts about what we expected from intimacy." She did not want casual acquaintances to know her former husband's problem. She was close to accurate, wouldn't you agree?

Setting the Record Straight

If you don't have a summary of your own, others will make up a story for you—and it won't necessarily have anything to do with what really happened. When my first husband and I divorced, a friend dropped over to talk to me about the divorce. He told me that he thought the whole problem was that my parents had given us too much stuff—trips, cars, a down payment on a house. He was certain that my parents' generosity caused our divorce. My soon-to-be-ex agreed that the friend was dead wrong. Their gifts had only provided us with more opportunities for enjoyment and freedom from anxiety. Our real problems were elsewhere.

If you don't give people a story they can wrap their minds around, they will automatically project onto you what is going on in their lives or what their values suggest is the problem. You may be thinking, "What does it matter what other people think?" On one hand, it's true:

What others think doesn't matter. On the other hand, we have to live in communities and in relationships with many people. Being able to communicate your point of view is part of life-mastery, whether it is about your divorce or the raise you want at work. This is just as good a time as any to practice standing up for yourself.

Releasing Your Feelings

Finally, constructing and sharing your story will help you develop an understanding of what happened, and this usually leads to being released from the power it has over you. Have you ever been angry with someone, told them how you felt, and then noticed that you really weren't that angry any more? Talking about feelings changes them. You are less likely to be stuck with your upset feelings if you create and share your story.

CREATING YOUR STORY

MOST OF us experience the death of marriage as a complex matter that we need to analyze. For better or for worse, in sickness and in health, you are going to have to create a story that helps you understand why the divorce occurred. Sometimes it's fairly simple. If your mate had a midlife crisis that led to an affair, for example, it may be easier to grasp what happened—"My husband left me for a younger woman because he was afraid of getting old." But you still may need to understand what the warning signs were that would have predicted this outcome early in the relationship. Other times, it's not clear initially what caused the divorce.

Cindy, a client of mine, took her two children to visit her mom for the weekend. When she came home, her husband, Jake, was gone—just like that. Jake had left a letter on the kitchen table telling her that he did not love her anymore and that he was filing for divorce. He did not leave a number where he could be reached. Cindy was taken completely by surprise. Where did this come from? She soon learned through friends that he was living with another woman, but he refused to speak to Cindy or his children. When Cindy came to see me three months later, she still had not seen Jake face-to-face. Cindy's first job in healing was to come to an understanding about why the relationship had ended. She had to construct her story of the divorce with almost no input from Jake.

Often you will have some kind of input from your ex, but it may not be honest or fair. For example, Kevin and Christine had been married for 10 years when Christine announced she was leaving. Kevin was devastated. How could she leave so suddenly, when they had agreed that they would work through any problem together? Christine replied, "You were always so strong. I couldn't be honest with you, because you always knew what you wanted and I didn't." This seemed like a lame excuse to Kevin, and he later learned that Christine had been having an affair for several months. This knowledge helped him come to a more complete picture of why Christine left.

Sometimes the true story does not reside in the other party's heart, but in your own. Gina and Ted appeared to have a normal, even happy, marriage. People were stunned when the two divorced. Gina cited all sorts of reasonable justifications—they had nothing in common, the sex was lousy, and his possessiveness was suffocating. But the truth was that she was afraid of her husband. In private, Ted would throw things, kick machines that frustrated him, and yell at her. Gina had spent their thirteen years together living in fear that he would lose control and beat her up. When she discussed her fears with Ted, he told her she was imagining things. She felt she couldn't talk to anyone else about his temper. To her, his rage and her fear were an awful secret. To make matters worse, she doubted herself enough to wonder if maybe Ted was right—she was being too sensitive. After all, he had never hit her or thrown anything at her. Gina's first step in healing was to face the truth and tell her story to herself and to someone else. In Gina's case, the "someone else" was a divorce group I conducted.

Tell Your Feelings

Truth is slippery. When you share your story, present a limited and accurate description—the shorter the better, and with no loaded emotional words. If Gina had said Ted was "abusive," someone might have wanted to debate her version of the story. When Gina said, "I was afraid of him," that was accurate. You know you have told the truth if you talk about one of two things. First, describe *your* feelings. Statements such as "I always felt frustrated" or "I felt so lonely in the marriage" are descriptions of how you felt. "He had to win" or "I was abandoned" are not descriptions of your feelings. Remember, however, feelings change. Tell your story about what you are feeling, but always with the knowledge that your feelings may not remain the same over time.

Stick with the Facts

I encourage people to give the least dramatic version of the demise of their marriage. There is a good reason for that. If you say the other person was a raving maniac, people may not believe you, particularly if you spent several years with your maniac. If you stick with the facts— "I came home and found her in bed with her old boyfriend"—then you know you have stated the truth. You will know you are accurate if you share a simple description of events.

Being accurate and factual should also decrease some of your obsessions about why the marriage ended. If you spend a great deal of time trying to assess who was most at fault, you will waste a lot of time. Basically, you need to be able to say, "This is what I know happened and this is how I felt," rather than feeling compelled to come up with a perfect analysis of how much blame should be allotted to you or your ex. If he or she had 64 percent of the blame and you had 36 percent, what difference does it make? It doesn't change the fact of the divorce.

GOING DEEPER:
WHY DID YOU CHOOSE YOUR EX?

YOUR MAIN goal is to construct a story about the divorce: What happened to cause the split? Sometimes, however, we want to go deeper and ask ourselves why we married this person in the first place. What can we learn from this so we won't make the same mistake next time? Part of constructing your story is taking the time to see what was good about the old marriage and what was bad.

When my 10-year marriage ended, my first thoughts were, "Well, there went 10 years down the drain." As time went on, I came to see what had led me to select him as my spouse, what had been good about the relationship, what I wanted to avoid in the future, and what I would want to include in a future relationship. Most important, I had to come to an understanding of why the marriage ended.

Linda came to therapy with me because she knew that she had to tell her story to someone. She had been married for 18 years, and all that time had been unable to function sexually. Finally, she and her husband divorced. When Linda entered therapy two years later, she felt that she couldn't just keep silent. From the time she was 11 years old until she left home, her father had sexually abused her. She had been afraid to sleep at night for fear she would awaken to his violating her. When Linda had tried to tell her mother the truth, her mom had told Linda she was lying, which confused the little girl even more. One month after high school graduation, Linda left home by marrying Jim. For 20 years, she didn't tell anyone the details of what had happened to her as a child.

Linda had a mediocre marriage outside the bedroom, but sexuality became impossible for her. Being intimate was associated with such violation and terror. Because she had survived at home by mentally separating from her body, acting as though the violations were happening to someone else, she was able to be sexual in a mechanical way for a number of years. Eventually, she was unable to have sex at all.

Since the divorce, her grief and anger over her childhood had begun to overwhelm her. "I just need to tell someone what actually happened. I told Jim that my father abused me, but I never told him any specifics of what my father did."

I was supportive, and began to reassure her with soothing phrases—"It wasn't your fault. You're not alone. Many women and some men too have faced this experience." Still, Linda could not tell me her childhood story. I thought this was very understandable, as she might need to know me better to trust me. I tried telling her a little of my life to reassure her that I was human and had experienced my own sadness, even though they were not childhood experiences. "Now she can trust me," I thought. But another session came and went without her telling me what had happened.

I tried other therapeutic strategies. I thought Linda might be feeling guilty about experiencing some pleasure during the violation, a common response of someone who has been abused. I offered her the understanding that our bodies can enjoy something our minds and spirits might reject. A biological response has nothing to do with the fact that she was being used unfairly. I waited, anticipating that this would reassure her. Still she could not tell me her story.

Eventually, I came up with the idea that if she could get some physical distance from me, it would be easier. I rearranged the room so her chair was facing away from me, and that was the key. I kept silent as she began to tell me about her father having sex with her. She described how painful it had been, and how he had confused her by saying loving things while hurting her. She told her story in a monotone, but at the end she began to cry, and I reassured her that I understood and she could take all the time she needed to cry. After several minutes of sobbing, Linda was ready to talk again. She looked lighter, as though her burden had lifted. She said, "My God! What a relief! It seems less horrible actually saying what happened than thinking about saying it."

Linda had finally gotten to tell her childhood story, and eventually she was able to fit her divorce into her difficult history. Her story boiled down to the simple fact that she could not be intimate with anyone until she dealt with her sexual abuse. She wisely chose a therapist to handle this kind of information. Over the next two years, she was able to establish a sexual relationship with a man who was patient and caring. She experienced sexual enjoyment, feeling herself to be in her body for the first time with her new partner.

Most of us have a less dramatic history than Linda's. Nonetheless, we still need to develop an understanding of how we chose the mate we did in the first place, so we don't keep creating the same story over and over. In Linda's case, any mate would have helped her escape from the hideous home life she was having. She did not need to figure out why she would have wanted to leave home. But most of us have more subtle motivations in picking our mates. We need to look back to the dating period and examine what, if anything, was going on then that planted the seed of the divorce years later.

Jerry told Pam before they were married that he was obsessed with sex. Pam loved sex too, so she thought this would not be a problem. But it was. After six years of marriage and two children, Pam became somewhat less interested in sex. Jerry spent much of his computer time online with sexually explicit material. On evenings he claimed to be working late, he was paying prostitutes to have sex with him. Since he was not willing to get help for his problem, Pam divorced him. Looking back, she could see that she chose to ignore the signs of impending doom that were there before she ever said "I do."

How many times have you met someone whose two or more previous spouses were either abusive (verbally or physically) or alcoholics? All too often, I suspect.

Listening to people's life stories in my therapy office, I am sometimes dismayed at how often they have repeated the same pattern—women who are attracted to take-charge, possessive men only to discover later that they are abusive; or men who seem to have a knack for finding needy, alcoholic women. Even when people have had two, or sometimes three, similar spouses, and the pattern is crystal clear to everyone else, logic doesn't prevail to keep them from marrying the same type of person over and over.

Barry was struggling with his second divorce when he came to see me. Both his wives had been vivacious and seductive, and both had cheated on him early in each marriage. Barry was the opposite: stodgy and introverted. Barry and I explored three goals in therapy: (1) identifying (and not ignoring) the early warning signs that he was picking out a woman who would be unfaithful; (2) developing the more free and open side of his character, which his wives had represented; and (3) participating in creating his next marriage, so he would not fall back into his old pattern again. Once Barry had accomplished these goals, I felt certain that he had the tools to make better choices in the future.

Some people repeat their stories, but many others choose a new mate who is opposite from their first, as an overreaction to their unhappiness. Elizabeth had divorced John because he "lacked ambition." A sweet guy, John was happy with his life and content to be a grocery clerk in a small town. Elizabeth wanted more. She took their three kids, moved to a large city, started a teaching career, and looked for a mate with more fire. She met Lee, a driven, up-and-coming executive. He fell passionately in love with her and they married. Eventually, his passion for her cooled and he became passionate about photography, restoring old cars, and motorcycles. She had been so intent on living a different life that she gave up all the contentment from her last marriage and chose someone too intense for her next marriage.

Therapists often strongly recommend not getting involved with another partner for at least one year—ideally, two—after a divorce. If Elizabeth had taken more time to develop a sense of contentment within herself, she might have made a less drastic shift. It is impossible not to seek a lover who completes you or adds something to your life that you lack; but the secret is to be sure you have thought through everything that will go with those characteristics. If you want someone who is ambitious, for example, be aware that you may be spending many nights alone.

WHO SHOULD YOU CHOOSE FOR A CONSULTANT?

CREATING YOUR story may sound easy, but it can be difficult. To get some perspective, it helps to have a consultant—someone who may have known you and your former spouse for a while and can help you develop an accurate picture. The question is, who is the best person to choose?

Not Your Ex!

I know it may be tempting to talk to your ex about what happened, but it's a bad idea for two reasons. First, your ex-spouse may have a very distorted view of you (and, if you think about it, you may have an equally distorted view of your ex). After all, he or she needs to develop a rationale for the divorce too. You might not be divorced in the first place if your ex thought well of you. I would not count on a former spouse's view of me. Having been married twice, I have had the chance to experience what is me and what was someone else's view of me. Each of my former partners describes me in a different way, and neither describes me in the way I would describe myself. Second, discussing your story creates intimacy. When you are trying to detach from someone, it is not the right time to be sharing your guts.

The exception to this no-spouse rule is when you need to make amends for your past actions. In the 12 steps that Alcoholics Anonymous recommends, one of the steps is to acknowledge your guilt to the person you have wronged. This is what Rick decided he had to do. Rick's wife had taken the kids and left three years before because she could no longer put up with his drinking. His drinking became much worse after the divorce, and eventually he hit bottom, opted for recovery, and joined AA. Through AA, Rick decided that he needed to tell his truth to his former wife and to his kids: that he had hurt his family and disrupted their lives through his drinking. When he could acknowledge what he had done, this left some room for his ex-wife and children to forgive him. Even though there could be no marital reconciliation, their relationship did improve so that the transition was easier for the children.

Occasionally, partners share their stories and patch up the marriage. Bill and Marcie were both in the military, and their marriage was touch and go. The mandatory tour of duty that separated them was a trial marital separation in their eyes. Bill and Marcie each confessed to me separately that they had had extramarital affairs, but that the other did not know this. My instincts told me this had to be out on the table, particularly since they seemed to have an equal score on betrayals. This took a great deal of courage, even for these two soldiers, but it allowed them to be truly close for the first time in their marriage. Once they had struggled to tell their truths, the barriers to closeness were eliminated.

Friends and Relatives

Friends and relatives are often a good choice. Don't plunge in without asking, however. Test the waters and see how a friend or relative feels about the story you are planning to share.

I was feeling cozy with an elderly relative while we were preparing a meal together. I had wanted to discuss the drinking problem of the man I had been dating for two years. But when I started to discuss the concept of alcoholism, she said, "That's just a moral weakness." That comment made me reconsider what I was about to tell her. What useful input was going to come from her, if she dismissed his problem as a moral weakness? I tried to fast-forward in my mind what recommendation might come from that statement. She might suggest prayer. I believe in prayer; in fact, I had already prayed about it many times. But I felt my partner was not going to respond well to my telling him "I think we need to pray about your drinking." I saved my concerns for my other friends, some of whom were therapists specializing in chemical dependency.

If you begin to tell your story and your friend says, "I don't want to take sides," assume that means the friend doesn't want to talk about your divorce. The take-sides statement may mean "There but for the grace of God go I," or "Don't upset me with emotions," or "I'm trying to stay friends with both of you." Change the subject, as there is clearly not an invitation for continuing the topic.

Even when you are telling someone who wants to listen, you still have to be selective. Ask yourself, "How does my friend feel about this topic and how does he or she usually resolve conflicts?" When I was going through my divorce, some friends were so angry with my former husband that just talking to them would tend to stir up my own upset. They were taking his behavior as personally as I did. One friend even wrote him a scathing letter. I knew those friends would help me construct a story that depicted my ex as a villain. Although you don't want to tell someone who will minimize your feelings, you also usually don't want to have gas tossed on your emotional flame.

When looking for your story consultant, ask yourself whose judgment you trust and who is known for moderation. Of course, there may be times when you need the energy of an upset friend to stand your ground with a bully. Being involved in a legal battle would be a good time to have a feisty friend in your corner. I had such a friend in my neighbor, who was my cheerleader as I went through divorce. Whenever I felt like giving up, I could count on her giving me the boost I needed to follow through with all the legal details that needed to be handled. Be aware of the effect of the listener's responses on you. Pick the person to share your story with based upon how he or she has reacted to similar disclosures.

Your Therapist

A story consultant might be a professional therapist. He or she may do more than just listen: Your therapist could help you develop your story. Having an uninvolved party give you feedback about your relationship, actions, or decisions allows you to shift perspective.

When Lillian came to see me, she had made peace with her husband's shortcomings. She had downplayed her irritations—which ranged from as mild as picky eating and not participating equally in the housework to his romantic involvement outside the marriage—feeling that commitment was more important than responding to petty differences. As her counselor, I repeatedly had to remind Lillian that most people would label her husband's actions at best as "not treating your spouse well" and at worst as "mental abuse." It was very hard for Lillian to see things from an outsider's point of view. Her commitment strategy of optimistically minimizing differences interfered with her ability to see the marriage for what it was. When she was able to grasp a different perspective, it was a crucial step toward making peace with the changes in her life.

Keep in mind, however, that therapists are human. They have issues that may act as filters through which they see your life and your relationships. It can happen that the issue the therapist brings up is not really yours in the first place. Margaret went to a therapist who interpreted everything in terms of control. If Margaret's ex offered to take the kids more often, if he sent the child support check early or late, if he commented on something he noticed needing repair around the house, it was all labeled by the therapist as an attempt to control. Margaret knew in her heart this wasn't right, so she changed therapists. Keep in mind that therapists can have their own axes to grind. You need to use your best judgment to decide if what they bring up is their issue or yours. After all, it is your story, not the therapist's, that you are paying to create.

Self-Help and Support Groups

Self-help and support groups may be a good place to tell your story. The only problem with self-help groups is that sometimes the group members may have an unconscious investment in your unhappiness. Social psychology teaches us that a group takes on a life of its own, and the group may begin to create subtle rules that keep it together. Ironically, the group's existence is threatened when members improve, so members may subtly undermine one another.

Sherry found this out when she announced to her Adult Children of Alcoholics (ACOA) group that she was going to leave. Group members began to suggest ways that she might be denying her identity as an ACOA. They suggested that her role with her boss—doing things that were beyond the call of duty—reflected her unresolved codependency. Someone else suggested that Sherry had never let herself get truly angry at her father for what his drinking did to their family. Pretty soon Sherry began to create a reality she had almost discarded—that she was a victim of her past and not likely to get much better. The group influenced how she constructed the story of her life.

In spite of these concerns, self-help groups, particularly time-limited ones that force you to resolve your issues within a deadline, can have value. It is valuable to have your feelings validated by others, to know you are not the only one suffering, and to receive input from others. Be cautious in your choice of groups and do not abandon your own good judgment.

Trust yourself and your intuition about who is worthy of hearing your story. If a one person doesn't react well, pick someone else who does. We all have wisdom inside. Take a moment to listen to it.

ALTERNATIVE WAYS TO TELL YOUR STORY

SOME PEOPLE find that they want to express themselves in other than the usual ways of simply talking about the history of the marriage. An alternative is to use your creativity.

My husband and I had written two books on marriage. Three months before we were to go on our ten-city book tour and be on the *Today* show to promote our newest book on marriage, he moved out. Within two months he was living with another woman. Telling my story was something I needed to do. Combining fun with fiction, I wrote a novel about my experiences in this unusual partnership. Writing this novel about my experiences was an important way for me to face the truth about what had happened. I released my anger through creativity, and also let go of a good portion of my grief.

One of my favorite mystery writers, Sue Grafton, says she began her mystery-writing career with *A Is for Alibi* when she went through a divorce and wanted to plan the perfect murder. Creativity can be a wonderful way to tell the truth about how you feel. I have often thought that it could be very healthy and liberating if we all took the time to write our autobiography. It would put things in perspective and lead us to a view of ourselves that might be more forgiving and comforting.

Don't stop with talking and writing, however. If you have other creative abilities, use those. My son Nick is the lead singer of the band 311. He told his story about the divorce by writing an angry song. Unlike most of us, who would privately hum our own little tune, his song "DLMD" is on a triple-platinum CD.

Consider any creative way to express your story. You may not be able to write it or sing it, but you might be able to sculpt or draw what has happened in the marriage. One day, Tiffany noticed that the clay her kids used turned to a less-attractive mud color when all the bright colors were combined. She decided to take the well-used clay and create a monster that represented how the marriage looked to her. She kept it on her chest of drawers in her bedroom to look at as she went through the legal process. A couple of times she smashed it and rebuilt the monster.

Any creative abilities you have can help you express your story. Creativity promotes movement in your life. Use yours!

IS YOUR STORY THE TRUTH?

IT IS hard to construct a true story if you do not *know* the true story. Often, as a relationship breaks up, there is a great deal of lying: "You slept with him!" "No I didn't!" "You blew all our money at the track!" "No I didn't!" It's often difficult to tell who is telling the truth. Sometimes one partner gets legal advice to keep his or her extra-marital relationship a secret. Occasionally, years later, people find out their "upstanding" ex-spouse was leading a double life as a pederast, an embezzler, or a con artist, and most of what they knew consisted of deliberate lies.

For all of these reasons, it may be difficult for divorcing people to have accurate data with which to create a true story about what led to the end of the marriage. Yet, for your peace of mind, you need to construct a story as honestly as you can. Most stories will be a mundane series of disappointments. So many couples have marriages that end because of unwillingness to deal with conflict, differences, or simply neglect of the relationship. When issues are left unspoken, marriages wither. It is not unusual to hear divorcing couples say, "We never had a fight." I am not proposing that fighting is good for a marriage, but if something is bothering you—in most long-term relationships, there will be something—you will have to deal with it if you want to have a happy relationship.

Things Change

Unfortunately, even if you and your ex were to agree on why the divorce occurred, you might change your minds later. Some dear friends of mine went through a divorce after seventeen years of marriage. At the end of that marriage, the wife said to her husband, "I don't think you ever loved me." He agreed. Four years later, when she had already married someone else, her former husband telephoned her to say that he had loved her, but he became immobilized when she asked for more intimacy.

The "truth" about feelings can change, depending on your vantage point at the time. It took a great deal of energy to get out of that marriage, and so the truth as they experienced it at the moment of divorce was that it had been a loveless marriage. With hindsight, they both saw that lack of love was not the truth. Ultimately, they were able to assess their marriage honestly, and agreed that they had lacked the skills to create intimacy and were unable to acquire those skills in therapy.

I recently bought a pin that has this saying on it: "The past is no more carved in stone than the future." All you can do is state what seems to be the truth as honestly as you can at the time, knowing that your perspective and story of the divorce may change.

STORIES THAT BOG YOU DOWN

TELLING YOUR story is one thing. Taking on your tale as the essence of you is another. Being stuck is the last place I would want to see you. State your truth, but don't become your own story of loss.

When Lisa came to see me, it was clear it had initially been helpful for her to attend a codependency group as part of her divorce recovery. After a while, however, she began to see every human interaction through that filter. She was no longer "Lisa who was helpful to her co-workers, who called her aging parents, who enjoyed her friends," she was "Lisa the Codependent." What may have started as a truth—"I felt codependent in my marriage"—became "I am codependent and that is all I am." She began to surround herself with friends who spoke the self-help language, and together they questioned every interaction. It was weirdly ironic to me that many of her long-term friends, who might have been dependent on her in the past, now avoided her because she had become such a walking lexicon of self-help jargon. I suppose getting people to avoid hearing you talk about codependency is one way to cure the codependency. Lisa's story was bogging her down.

You are much more than any event or sum of many events. You have choices. That is the dilemma and the thrill of being a person. Whether you tell a therapist, a friend, or family member, there is some learning that happens when you are able to tell your story. Your perspective changes by hearing yourself tell your story and by feedback from others. Acknowledge your story to yourself, find somebody to tell it to, and get on with your life.

The Way of the Story

In order to move on with your life, you need some way to wrap your mind around this life-changing event. Your explanations for why your marriage ended may change over time, but creating the story—the explanation—of the divorce is still a necessity.

WHY DO I NEED A STORY?
- The brain insists on creating stories
- To avoid physical illness

- To permit ease of social interactions
- Others are interested
- To provide closure
- To avoid repeating the same situation (warning signs)
- To avoid jumping from the frying pan into the fire
- To recognize the ongoing saga of your life

WHERE DO I GET
THE DATA TO CONSTRUCT
MY STORY?
- Not from your ex
- From friends and relatives who have known your marriage
- From your therapist
- And from your own knowledge

WHO CAN I USE FOR A
SUPPORTING CONSULTANT?
- Your therapist
- Friends and relatives
- Groups
- Rarely your ex, except for facts, such as dates of events

(continued)

The Way of the Story–continued

HOW CAN I TELL MY STORY
BESIDES TALKING?
- Write a story
- Compose a song
- Draw a picture
- Make a sculpture

TRUTH OR FICTION?
- Your story may change over time
- Don't become your story

CHAPTER TWO

Heal Your Imagination

I like the dreams of the future
better than the history of the past.
—THOMAS JEFFERSON

WHEN I was going through my first divorce, I had a dream I was telling an old family friend that I was divorced. The family friend was Bud Taylor, a farmer in Tennessee who represented family and stability to me. In the dream I looked next to where I was sitting and saw a young girl crying. My interpretation was that the young girl represented the young, optimistic part of me, who had dreams of the life she would share with her husband.

Even if you want the divorce and feel mostly relieved by the ending of the marriage, you still need to face the death of the dreams you had going into the marriage. Your imagination has had a traumatic blow. It must be healed as part of the recovery process. Step two in our 7-step method is to heal your imagination.

The imagination is that part of us that gives us hope by creating images of the future, peace by allowing us to picture calming scenes, and relief by creating images that put the past far behind us. Often people associate the imagination with what their third-grade teacher told them to do: Stop daydreaming. But in this case, daydreaming is the source of additional healing. Without this internal resource, you may suffer from divorce longer than necessary. So take an experimental attitude toward this resource and see how much it can add to your recovery.

We are going to explore three specific ways to use your imagination to speed your healing process: Sending off your past through imagery, healing your present through relaxing images, and rejuvenating your future through creating successful future images. Keep in mind that whatever you concentrate on tends to expand: If you dwell on the gloom of your divorce, your interior space will be filled with murky images. But if you imagine a better future, those optimistic thoughts will take up more space in your life. Your ability to control what goes through your mind is an essential skill in healing from a divorce and creating success in your life.

HEALING YOUR PAST

FOR OVER 50 years, my father was a therapist who helped people cope with all sorts of problems, including divorce. One of his favorite ways to help people get over the past was to use imagery. He would ask his clients to put their images of their no-longer-useful memories in a boat, a rocket ship, or a hot-air balloon and launch them. Recently, I was having lunch with a minister friend of mine named Katy. As I talked to her about this technique, she said, "I've been using that for years too. I have called it prayer." Whether you think of this as prayer, guided imagery, self-hypnosis, or daydreaming, here is how to use it for yourself.

Find a comfortable place where you will not be disturbed for the next hour. Allow yourself to unplug the telephone. Sit in your easy chair or lie down. You are welcome to have a clock in view, so you can peek at it and keep track of time. After you have the proper setting, you can begin to focus internally. Take three deep breaths, and imagine breathing in peace and exhaling tension with each breath. Now think of the most relaxing place you can imagine—either a place you have been or a place you can imagine visiting, such as a beautiful garden. Use your senses to place yourself in a scene. Think of what you would see (trees, the ocean, sunlight), hear (running water, birds, the breeze), smell (flowers, grass, leaves), and feel (the air on your skin, the feeling of the water flowing through your fingers, and the warmth of the sunlight on your body). Paint as vivid a picture as you can of your relaxing place.

People often ask me to give them a script to follow for such occasions. If you like the beach, this guided visualization may be the one for you:

Take three deep breaths. As you inhale, say to yourself, "Breathe in peace." As you breathe out, say, "Exhale tension." As you exhale the third time, allow your body to slump. Allow any outside noises to be a signal for you to become more relaxed and comfortable. Now imagine being on the beach. Notice the sounds of the waves as they come in with a roar and the soft musical sound as they go out over and over again. Notice the smell of the salty water as you feel the healing warmth of the sun on your skin. Look out over the water and notice how the ocean is different colors in different places and how the sunlight dances upon the water. Notice the smell of your favorite sunscreen and the moist feeling on your skin. Notice the sounds of birds near the beach and look out over the ocean. You might see a seagull catching the wind in her wings and just remaining lazily suspended in the air. Notice the sounds of people playing on the beach in the distance and the sounds of the wind coming off the ocean. Reach down and pick up a handful of warm sand and feel the tickling sensation of it flowing between your fingers, noticing how each grain is different. Notice the moist warmth of the sea breeze as it lightly moves the hair on your body. Let yourself feel one with nature and at peace.

Letting Go of the Past

Whatever you choose—the beach, the woods, the mountains, your own bedroom, a lovely garden—your goal is to use your ability to relax and to let the creative part of you help you heal. Now you are ready to let go of the disturbing images from the past. If you have visualized a river or an ocean, you can imagine sending your ex off in a boat. If you were in a garden or a meadow, you can imagine sending your ex off in a hot-air balloon. Watch the boat or the balloon until it floats completely out of sight. You may remember having a helium-filled balloon escape from you and watching it float away. After staring at the departing balloon, you eventually were not sure you still saw it. In your imagination, watch it past that time until the sky or water seems empty.

If you have some spiritual or religious images that you can use with your imagery experience, you will find them helpful. You might want to add a religious aspect by picturing a particular spiritual figure, such as Jesus, Mohammed, Buddha, or the Dalai Lama, helping you push the boat off the shore. If you do not want a religious image, you could include a favorite person, living or dead, such as a grandparent.

You may want to send away a scene rather than a person—for example, the sight of your ex with his or her lover. Or maybe you want to dispose of a series of scenes, such as the multiple times you discovered that your ex was gambling. One way to do this is to imagine sitting in a movie theater and watching a documentary of the demise of your marriage. Look at it objectively. As the movie ends, see the words "The End" on the screen. Imagine seeing the movie run fast in reverse, so that you can feel that the feelings are all contained in that reel of film. See yourself begin to exit the theater and go to the lobby. There you can find that reel of film with all the memories and the power those experiences have had over your life. Imagine taking that reel of film out to the parking lot and burning the movie in a bonfire. Watch the smoke rise as you let all the power those memories had over your life rise with it.

Martin used this technique to let go of his wife, Janelle. She had become a compulsive gambler and would secretly withdraw money from their joint account. After repeated attempts to get her into therapy or Gamblers Anonymous, he had to divorce her to save himself from financial ruin. He imagined seeing a movie of the many times he had caught her gambling after her repeated vows that she would not gamble anymore. On his imaginary screen, he saw their many tearful fights. He saw himself reading their bank statement, which provided proof she was lying again about gambling. When he imagined burning the movie, he felt that some physical weight was removed from his body. Because they had no children, he would probably never have to see Janelle again. Using his imagination made the divorce emotionally final, since all the legal matters had been handled. It was likely that Martin would still feel sad again in a nostalgic way, but most likely his anguish was now over.

I always like to put something positive in the place of something negative that I am sending away. In the place of painful discoveries in my divorce, I put confidence in my future and a spiritual image of receiving a blessing.

Maria was a good Catholic wife who had four grown children and a daughter and two sons about to leave home. Her husband might have been diagnosed as a voyeur with a midlife crisis. He had left her for a woman 25 years younger than he, but not before it was discovered that he had been watching their daughter through a hole in the wall as she changed her clothes. Maria was disgusted and felt that all men were slime. She knew she had to get over this feeling for the sake of her two sons. Because of her faith, I had her picture Jesus coming to her and saying something that would ease her pain and rage toward men. I saw a visible change in her face as she went through the process. Her tension seemed to melt away. When she opened her eyes after the imagery, she reported that Jesus had said to her, "Remember, I am a man too." Some years later, she told me that imagery was a turning point for her and she hoped I would tell other people her story.

HEALING THE PRESENT

ONCE YOU have let go of the past, you can begin to heal the present. You can apply the same relaxation techniques, but this time you will send yourself healing energy.

I like to imagine a healing light flowing into each cell in my body. I start with my scalp, and imagine light filling every cell of my scalp. (I have wondered if this could be a treatment for dandruff!) Then I imagine the light filling my face, starting with my forehead and working down. I go over each part of my body and each organ, imagining the healing light filling every cell until I am filled with healing.

Here is a script you might use:

Imagine yourself sitting on a hill overlooking a green valley. Below are fields of different crops in different shades of green. In the center of the valley is a lazy stream that makes a ribbon of light as the sun shines on the water. Smell the grass, the leaves, the moist smell of earth, as the gentle breeze from the valley floor caresses your body. Notice the blue of the sky and a few clouds in the distance. As you look at the clouds, notice one intense beam of light shining through the cloud. That beam of light begins to move from the cloud across the fields and toward you. As the beam of light reaches you, you feel a comfortable safety in the warmth of the light. It shines on your head, sending healing light into each cell of your scalp.

As it fills your scalp, the healing light makes any alterations in muscle tension, blood flow, or biochemistry that would improve your health and comfort. The light fills each cell in your forehead and your sinuses. It changes blood flow and biochemistry and makes any changes necessary for your health. Then the light fills your jaw, your gums, and your entire face so that every cell is adjusted in a way that is exactly appropriate for your health. The light then fills your brain. If there are any minute alterations that need to be made in the little substances between each nerve in your brain for your physical and mental health, those changes can occur now.

The light has now filled every cell in your head and begins to shine down through your neck, again adjusting any muscle tension for your neck to be comfortable. Then the light fills your insides, starting with your bronchial tubes and shining into your lungs, making any adjustment in smooth muscle tension, any cleansing, any biochemical changes that are necessary for your health. The light flows over to your heart, adjusting the muscle of your heart in a way that is exactly appropriate to your health. The healing light flows down your aorta and into your spleen, your liver, your gall bladder, your stomach, your intestines, your kidneys, and reproductive system, again making any necessary adjustments for your health and comfort.

The light flows down your shoulders and out to your arms, wrists, and fingertips. The healing light then flows down your spinal column, one vertebra at a time, making any adjustments and particularly adjusting each disk in a way that is appropriate for your health and comfort. The healing reaches your tail bone and spreads out to your hips, making any adjustments along the way that will promote your health and your comfort. Then the healing light flows through your legs, particularly filling your knees and making any changes in muscle tension or fluids to make your knees as healthy as possible. The light flows down to your ankles and all the way out to the tips of your toes.

As you enjoy the sense of every cell being cleansed and adjusted, you can let that light concentrate in your solar plexus and be there for you any time you need it for health and comfort.

This script is a way for you to have a sense of peace and spiritual healing without necessarily focusing on a religious image. If you prefer a religious tone, simply substitute the power of a deity for all the light images. To begin practicing relaxing imagery, you may want to record this script and play it for yourself when you want to relax. (I have tapes available for you too. Please see pages 167–168.)

From time to time, when one part or another of my body seems to need the healing light, I focus on that area.

For example, I imagined light from God shining into my chest and healing what felt like a broken heart after my husband left. I experienced a real shift after that imagery, and felt open to the possibility of loving someone again. This combination of prayer and imagery is a very powerful way to heal.

Use Your Imagination to Prevent Automatic Reactions

Sometimes circumstances will dictate that you must see your former spouse repeatedly—for the sake of the children, for example, or for business reasons, such as the 10-city book tour I had to go on with my former husband. It's easy to fall into the same old emotional reactions, but it's not necessary. How can you use your imagination to not react? There are two ways: You can imagine your ex surrounded by something, such as a wall or a cage. Or you can imagine yourself surrounded by a clear bullet-proof, insult-proof shield.

When Ginger had to go on a business trip with her soon-to-be ex, she came to me for some ideas about how to protect herself from him emotionally. I suggested she put herself in a relaxed state every night before she went to bed and that she picture a wall around him. In her imagination she could see him surrounded by a clear, four-inch-thick shield. This reminded her that he could not get to her; and that no matter what he said, she did not have to react. The image allowed her to be calm and finish the work they had to do together.

Meredith lived in a small farming community, where both family and friends had opinions about her and her ex, and criticism of her for divorcing. To protect herself, she imagined that she was surrounded by a magic bubble of thick acrylic that nothing could penetrate. To test the effectiveness of her shield against verbal attacks, she decided to imagine the family throwing rotten tomatoes at her shield. She watched them hit the acrylic and slowly slide harmlessly down the sides of the shield. She found whenever she encountered relatives she was able to be slightly amused at the tomato image and her lack of reaction to criticism.

REJUVENATING YOUR FUTURE

SO FAR, we have discussed how you can use your imagination to get over a divorce by healing your past or healing and calming your present. However, you can even use your imagination to heal your future. Many divorcing people may not even realize the dreams they had about the future of the marriage until a divorce forces them to give up those dreams. Although living in the present is desirable, healing or revising your images of the future is crucial to recovery from a divorce.

Monica had been married for 20 years. The divorce hit her like a ton of bricks. She had been a homemaker, devoted to her three children. She had graduated many years ago with a degree in English but had never held a job. When Don left, she was completely lost. We first worked on the skills she needed to manage a budget and get a job. After a few months she began work as a receptionist at a bank. There was hope for advancement, and her settlement included some alimony and plenty of child support. She was surviving. But Monica was still grieving over Don, who had since remarried. She was dreading the holidays. "We have so many cherished traditions. So many happy memories. How can Christmas ever be fun again?"

I asked Monica to close her eyes for a guided visualization. I described a relaxing place, and had her picture a Christmas five years from now. Her oldest daughter would be home from college, her son would be a teenager, and her youngest starting middle school. I asked her to picture a delicious meal, with laughter and stories from the children's lives and maybe extra guests—family or new friends. Once Monica was able to picture some point in the future where she would not feel so miserable, she had hope. She was able now to go forward with less pain.

Why did I pick a point far on the horizon? Because I felt that she would not believe me if I told her the Christmas after next would be much better (even though I thought it would). But hope is what keeps us going. In *The Alchemist,* a charming little allegory about following your dreams, Paul Coelho writes, "It's the possibility of having a dream come true that makes life interesting."

Recently, I became a grandmother for the first time. This was literally a dream come true. The anticipation that someday I would have another little person to love was one of the images I used to pull me forward in 1994 when my husband left. Imagining holding that baby, taking a toddler to the beach, experiencing the world fresh through that child's eyes—these were images I deliberately practiced to remind myself that there would be wonderful times in the future and new experiences.

Having dreams for yourself will pull you forward through your divorce adjustment. Sometimes you can pull your future images from the past. For instance, Mark had married in his thirties. Now, at 47, he was divorcing. I asked him, "Were you miserable before Luann came along?"

"No, I had a good life. Friends and my business. I was pretty happy," Mark recalled.

"Couldn't you be happy like that again? Think of what you did then and imagine doing some of those things now." This simple suggestion made a big difference for Mark.

Sometimes, rarely, this doesn't work. Greg and his wife married right after high school. They were just beginning the divorce process when I asked how his life was before Susan. Greg said, "Dr. Hudson, I have known Susan since the second grade!" So much for the how-was-your-life-before images! Eventually, I had Greg focus on the things he enjoyed that had nothing to do with his wife, such as fishing and hunting.

New Beginnings

In psychology, we know that you cannot do anything you cannot imagine yourself doing. The reverse is also true: If you can think it, you can do it. Divorce can be a great opportunity for a new beginning. The first step is to imagine that new beginning, whether it's living in an apartment instead of having the burden of a house, buying something you love without fear of criticism from your ex, or taking that art class you never had time for.

Divorce also gives people time and opportunity to begin thinking about a career change or a move. I had always wanted to live someplace warmer than Nebraska. After my divorce was final for a year, I moved my parents and my two sons from Omaha to the Dallas–Fort Worth area. I had imagined this for many years, and my divorce gave me the opportunity to do it.

Harriet had been married for 37 years when she divorced her husband, Charley, who had a drinking problem. Her two kids were grown. Now, for the first time, she could fulfill her dreams. She had worked in a hospital food service job and had achieved some success there, but her dream had always been to serve in the Peace Corps. When President Kennedy first announced the program, she had too many family obligations to go. Now was her chance. She wanted to travel and truly know how people lived elsewhere. At 58, she left for Peru to teach in a vocational school and help in a small community 50 miles from Lima. This was a dream she could never have fulfilled when she was married. Divorce gave her the chance to live her dream. You may want to think of something that you have always wanted to do. There is freedom without the obligations of marriage.

You don't have to pursue major dreams to enjoy the benefits of being single again. I found that little pleasures such as being able to go for ice cream when I wanted, eating whatever I wanted, or staying up late or sleeping in without having to take a mate into consideration were tiny pleasures that added to my dreams of a full life after divorce. While I like to live in the present, I know that there are always possibilities for future pleasant surprises ahead of me.

Life has compensations. This may be your chance to do what you have always wanted. Imagine it, make an action plan, and start the ball rolling.

Whatever You Concentrate On Expands

You can't just turn off the pain when your life has been turned upside down by divorce, but you can make an effort to control your focus.

Imagining that you will never be happy again is a good way to have depression expand. Imagining that you may be happier than you have ever been before is a good way to have happiness fill your life. Noticing what is great about your life now is a good way to have your heart fill with gratitude for the good in the present.

Marge decided to think of one thing that she was happy about or grateful for each time she ate anything. She did not think in terms of a prayer before eating, just a pause. The food would be her reminder to focus on positive aspects of her life since her divorce. As she spent her time thinking about what she liked in her life, she found herself feeling that her life was good. She liked her job, she had good friends, her parents loved her and were supportive—she found the list of good things far outweighed the list of disappointments from her divorce.

Einstein said, "Believing is seeing." As you focus on what is going right instead of what is going wrong, a good life will expand before you.

Imagination Regenerates Your Dreams

If you can imagine it, you can do it. We have known for over 30 years that imagination is a first step in creating change. Imagery can be used to heal the past, create healing images in the present, or rehabilitate the future.

TO HEAL YOUR PAST
THROUGH IMAGERY:
- Create send-off images
- Replace painful thoughts of the past with hope or comfort from spiritual images

TO INSTILL PEACE
IN THE PRESENT
THROUGH IMAGERY:
- Create a relaxing retreat in your mind
- Use healing light imagery

(continued)

Imagination Regenerates
Your Dreams–continued

To heal the future
through imagery:
- Remember that damaged dreams of the
  future are a big part of the loss in divorce
- Imagine a success point in your future
- Remember that whatever you concentrate
  on tends to expand, and replace painful images
  with pleasurable ones

CHAPTER THREE

Celebrate Divorce

The hardest thing in life
is to learn which bridges to cross
and which to burn.
—DAVID RUSSELL

W E HAVE ceremonies to mark life transitions and to symbolically express the change that is taking place. We've all been to birthday parties, retirement parties, marriages, and funerals. But if there is ever a time you need a way to mark a major change in your life, it's when you go through a divorce.

Unfortunately, our society does not have ceremonies for divorce. Organized religion rarely offers such an opportunity, perhaps because most faiths do not want to appear to condone the breakup of a marriage. Nonetheless, people going through the event need a way to mark the transition from couple to single.

Forming a marital union is usually a gradual transition—spending more and more time together, eventually living together. The engagement is announced and marked by a party, followed by showers and bachelor parties that remind the couple the transition is occurring. Then the ceremony of the legal and spiritual union is followed by a trip that marks the beginning of their life together—the honeymoon. Divorce, on the other hand, may be a spirit-jarring change: In a few minutes you go from being with one person every day for many years to not seeing that person at all.

Just as a weddings exist as a symbol of the transition into partnership, you can create your own "funeral" for the end of the partnership. The ceremony consists of (1) symbolic objects that represent the old marriage; (2) an action that symbolizes letting go of the old marriage, such as burning or burying a marriage license; (3) a symbol of a positive new "replacement" for the marriage, such as a vow to protect and love yourself; and (4) an action of closure, such as a cleansing and/or a celebration. Make the ceremony special: Select an emotionally significant place to hold it; wear special clothes, as you did for your wedding; and eat and drink foods that are special or represent the change for you.

I wish I could tell you that if you do this, your hurt, anger, or disappointment will be over instantly. I can't. The secret of creating a ritual that does change how you feel is doing the background work properly. Take time to prepare emotionally. Don't rush the ceremony. I often see clients who try to rush the divorce recovery by doing ceremonies before their time. You can't have a funeral for a relationship that is still on life support. But when the marriage is truly over, the court says so and so does your behavior, then it is time for a ceremony.

Since no real rituals exist, you are free to create your own—use what you wish and do what you wish! First we'll look at the elements you can use in your divorce ritual. Then we'll look at the distinct moments of divorce you may want to mark in your transition to a new life.

CHOOSE A SYMBOL

WE'RE ALL familiar with the primary symbol of the wedding ceremony—a ring to represent the unbroken pledge of commitment. Now that commitment is broken, and you will need to select a symbol to represent what you are letting go of and that you will not hold on.

You are going to ask yourself two questions: "What represents the marriage or its end?" and "What action would be the action of letting go?" The act of selecting a symbol and the thought you devote to the method of getting rid of it are part of the emotional work of healing from the divorce. The object you select may determine the action you take. For example, burning a golf ball might be hard work, but burying it or throwing it in the ocean could be easy. If you like burning things—as one who loves flambé, this is my favorite disposal method—you will need flammable objects such as old love letters, marriage licenses, pictures, or unsent letters you create. Let's consider items that already exist. They are the easiest to find.

Use an Existing Symbol

The end of a marriage creates a lot of symbolic items—copies of papers filed, receipts from motels that revealed an affair, empty liquor bottles, letters saying "I'm leaving," or pictures from an unhappy vacation that was your last trip together. The symbol may be the evidence of your spouse's betrayal. (Experts on affairs tell us that in 86 percent of divorces, a third party is involved, so marriages that end without betrayals are the exception.) Charlie knew his wife had cheated on him when he discovered the cellular telephone bills with the calls to New Hampshire where the other man lived. He called information to verify that the number belonged to the man with whom his wife had been involved, and used the receipt in his ceremony.

Receipts for gifts such as flowers, diamond earrings, or motel rooms are excellent ceremonial symbols of the ending of the marriage. Marlene knew that Steve had cheated on her when she found a charge for a jewelry store on the credit card, and knew she hadn't bought anything. She called to verify the purchase, and discovered they were for diamond earrings. She waited another month to receive them, just in case these were a surprise for her, but the gift was not for her. Later, she recalled that event as the beginning of the end of her marriage and used the receipt in a ceremony when the divorce was final.

Marriage licenses, divorce papers, pictures, letters to the other man or woman, all abound as symbols to be used in ceremonies. If you are concerned that you might later need those for legal reasons, make photocopies to destroy.

Create a Symbol

Creating symbols is therapeutic in itself. If you have any artistic talents—in fact, even if you don't—you may still create something artistic that represents your former marriage. You can make a collage of pictures from the marriage. You can make a sculpture out of clay or draw a picture that represents the marriage. The variations are infinite.

Marianne drew a downward spiral that represented the end of her marriage. At various points on the spiral, she drew symbols of the marriage's decline: a beer can, a wrecked car, a dollar sign to represent money troubles, and a sheriff's badge to represent calling the police. Marianne lived in a rural area and used a burn barrel for waste disposal, and she decided she would burn her drawing in the barrel the night after her divorce was granted in court. Her only regret in creating this symbol was that she had not drawn it on larger paper so it would take longer to burn.

Creating a symbol can also mean imbuing an object with ritual meaning—a rock representing the weight of the old relationship is perfect. I often encourage clients to find a rock that is heavy, but not so heavy that they cannot carry it around in a purse or briefcase for a week before they get rid of it. I also suggest they paint the rock black to symbolize mourning—a suggestion I learned from a psychologist friend, Jeff Zeig. If you carry the rock with you for a week before the ceremonial event, the ritual will be even more powerful.

Cliff felt particularly unsupported by his family, fundamentalist Christians who believed there was no reason good enough to get a divorce. When Cliff took his children and left his alcoholic wife, his family did not support his leaving. His rock—which he painted red and black for anger and mourning—represented both his disappointment and sadness about his marriage and his feelings of abandonment by his parents. When he dropped the children off to visit his parents, he put the rock under a shrub in their front yard to represent leaving their problem with them.

Rocks offer many disposal options. Now, now—I do not mean throwing it through your ex's window. You can find a body of water to throw it in. You can bury it in a yard. You can put it out in nature as a symbol of return to its primal state. If you live near a canyon or a rock quarry, somewhere where there is a vast expanse to heave the rock into, that might be a good option. If you are steady and strong of hand, you might use a chisel to break it into smaller pieces and then dispose of it.

Letters are another very popular form of created symbolism. When you write a letter, it feels as if you are moving your feelings outside yourself and onto the paper. My friend and business manager, Rhonda, was helping me clean out my desk for my move to Texas. She discovered a very angry letter I had written to my ex, and said, "This is burning my fingers. What do you want me to do with this?" When I saw what it was, I said, "Just throw it in the trash. I don't even want to touch it. I got rid of those feelings a long time ago. I would hate to get anger cooties on me again."

Buy a Symbol

Your third symbol-selection option is to purchase a special object that represents this transition. Lena kept feeling that all the symbols she had just weren't right. She knew that her marriage had died from neglect—her husband had filled up his weekends with golf and she had filled up her life with her friends, until the marriage took on the quality of an arrangement. She decided to buy a package of golf balls, bury it in the backyard, and put a little cross on the grave.

When Amelia's husband was having an affair with a neighbor, he had purchased a clear plastic key chain with the woman's name on it as a gift. Amelia felt that she needed to buy an identical key chain to vent her anger on as a preparation for her ceremony. She expressed her anger on the identical key chain by hammering on it, but that didn't feel like enough. So Amelia put it in the street in front of the neighbor's house and drove over it. That act made her ready to bury the remains of the key chain, and her rage at her ex-husband and the neighbor with it.

Jerry's wife had started the midlife crisis that ended their marriage by having cybersex. She progressed to having phone sex, and eventually real sex, with a man she met on the Internet. One day, while browsing at a novelty shop, Jerry saw a refrigerator magnet shaped like a tiny computer. He thought, "What a perfect symbol of what has happened to me." When he had his ceremony, he combined the symbol of the computer with a copy of his marriage license, burying them together.

CHOOSE A LOCATION FOR YOUR CEREMONY

WHETHER YOUR symbol is created, purchased, or already exists, selecting it is your first step in planning a ceremony. Finding a method and place to dispose of it is your next step. Your disposal method will help determine the location of your ceremony, but you might find that you end up in a couple of places as part of your ritual. Many people like to include a trip or an outing into nature as part of their ceremony. I have done a ceremony by a creek so that I could throw the ashes in the creek. (Is the Environmental Protection Agency going to be after me?)

Jean and Tom had been a couple who loved the outdoors—in fact, he had proposed to her on a trip to Estes Park, in Colorado. To close the circle of their marriage, she selected that location for her divorce ceremony. That night, she made a campfire and burned some mementos of their marriage. Then she performed a Native American-based ceremony, calling on the spirits in nature to give her power to heal and go on. Finally, to indicate she was going on with her life, Jean planned a little get-together back home to celebrate with the friends who were currently in her life.

Many women and some men say that when they got married they "stopped being themselves." Going someplace that made you happy as a child can be a nice way to recapture your true self as you go through divorce. Going back to your hometown is another good way to think and act in terms of finding yourself again. Even though it might be embarrassing to connect with high-school friends just as you are divorcing, it might also be a way to remember yourself outside of your role as husband or wife.

Another option is to look to the future as you leave the past behind: Perform your ceremony somewhere you have always wanted to visit but never did. Sue had always wanted to go to the Swiss Alps, and she had some extra money available from the divorce. She lugged her marriage license, some pictures, and a letter from the other woman all the way to Europe and burned them on a fabulous mountain.

The location you choose is up to you: the home you shared with your husband or wife, a symbolic location of your childhood, a place that feels victorious, or a private place such as your bedroom. The important point is to choose a location that adds meaning to your ritual.

DECIDE WHO TO INVITE

MOST DIVORCE rituals are, and should be, performed alone. The benefits of your ceremony may help others discover what they might do to heal on their own.

A divorce ceremony is a solitary experience because grief is a solitary experience. When someone dies, for example, you face the grief alone even if others are also grieving about the loss. Brothers and sisters, in spite of emotional closeness, report they still feel that they are going through the loss of a parent alone. The nature of the relationship between each child and a parent is so unique that the grief is unique too. Likewise, grieving about the divorce is unique to the two parties involved.

It might be argued that the children of the marriage are being "divorced" and should be part of the ceremony. I did not include my children in my own divorce ceremonies, but they knew that I was doing these things to move on and that they could do their own personal ceremonies. My oldest and youngest sons eventually performed their own symbolic tasks. The oldest wrote a song about his anger over the divorce, and the youngest burned something about the visitation he resented. Generally, I do not advise including children in your personal ceremony.

Occasionally, a divorcing couple may be so civilized and cordial that they could do a ceremony together when the divorce was final, although I have not personally known such a couple. I do, however, know of one couple who had been married for a very long time. Their friends were very upset over their divorce. When they moved out of the house they had lived in together, they had a "house-cooling party," as opposed to a housewarming party. Their friends came and helped them load separate trucks with the stuff each spouse was taking. That, in itself, was a ceremony and a way for everyone to make peace with the divorce.

MAKE A NEW VOW

IN A divorce ritual it is important not only to remove something or let something go, but to put something new in its place. When I do guided imagery with clients, if they send away anything from the past, I have them add self-confidence, compassion, or something of a spiritual nature in the mental void left by the removal of the painful memory. If you have to let go of your marriage vows, replace them with a vow to yourself, a spiritual being, your children, or even a future mate.

Betsy was a successful professional who had put up with way too much in her marriage. Her husband would not work steadily, yet he insisted on having control of the finances so he could buy what he wanted. He did little of the daily care of the children. He spoke unkindly to Betsy and was demanding, and she tolerated all of it. Finally, he was unfaithful, which was too much of a violation for her to continue the marriage. As the divorce proceeded, Betsy was furious with herself for putting up with all she had. She had contorted herself for this unworthy man. When she performed the ceremonial burning of a copy of her marriage license, she took a vow to protect herself and never allow anyone to take advantage of her the way her husband had. She wrote her vow on paper and displayed it in her bathroom where she would see it everyday. She prayed for wisdom to be able to see when she was being too tolerant.

Bob was visiting his mother when he found the tiny license plate that he had on his bike as a boy. He decided he would include it in his ceremony the night his divorce was final. First, he burned the letter to his ex-wife that he had been writing for the last month. Then he held the little license plate that said "Bobby" on it, and vowed not to let the happy energy of that little boy be crushed by the disappointment of the divorce. He found a special place to put the license plate where he would see it daily, a reminder to keep his happy childhood energy within him.

My friend Rachel married *herself* as part of her divorce, and vowed never to divorce herself or be untrue to herself. Even if she remarries externally, internally she will remain faithful to herself. This is a great symbol of personal integration.

Suzanne had allowed her husband to nearly ruin her financially. I suggested that she watch *Gone with the Wind* and take the vow that Scarlet O'Hara does when she holds up a root she is eating in desperation to avoid starving. She says, "As God is my witness, I will never be hungry again!" I thought Suzanne might say, "As God is my witness, I will never let anyone else control my money again." She felt better when she did this, although it took her four years to turn herself around financially.

Affirmations, vows, or special prayers can and should be part of any ceremony. Vows can be combined with prayer for support or protection. A prayer such as "Let the love of God surround and protect me in all my future dealings with the opposite sex" might be enough, but something spiritual and positive should be part of your ceremony. The more you can combine the transition ceremonies with a time of contemplation and religious integration of the experience, the greater the closure will be for you.

I want to clarify my use of the words spiritual and religious. You may have met people who respond to a question such as, "Are you religious?" with the answer, "I am spiritual, not religious." You may even say this yourself. I investigated the origin of the word religion and found that it comes from the Latin *religare,* meaning "to bind back, to bind man and the gods." I have concluded from this that if you are seeking a union with a Higher Power, no matter what organized doctrine may or may not be involved, then you are religious. The definition of spiritual is "of the spirit or the soul, often in a religious or moral aspect as distinguished from the body." We tend to use the word spiritual to imply an attempt to be better people, to consider a larger picture of the effect of our actions on others, and to take the soul into consideration as we make our decisions—all of which are good goals to have in creating ceremonies. Whichever word you use is fine with me, but now you know how I define the use of those two words.

While ridding yourself of something is good, filling yourself with something positive and strong is even better. Lisa burned a picture of her wedding as part of her divorce, which ended a three-year marriage. She included in her ceremony the statement, "Divine wisdom fills every decision I make about men." She wrote this on a piece of paper and put it in her makeup drawer in her bathroom, where she would see it every time she put on her makeup.

CLEANSING

BATHING TO wash away something always seems like a great idea to me. Maybe it's because I was raised in a religious tradition that believed in baptism by immersion. But for whatever reason, I think water is the greatest healing substance. In creating divorce ceremonies, people often include bubble baths; showers; a swim in a lake or river; going to hot springs; or sitting in the ocean at high tide, letting the waves wash over them, and then watching the water recede. You could even pour a pitcher of water over yourself on a warm day.

After burning wedding vows and cards from my ex, I took vows about loving myself and my youngest son, who was most affected by the divorce. I followed this with a reading of the Twenty-Third Psalm. Then I took a bath with bath oil in a tub surrounded by candles, to symbolize the uniqueness of the occasion. As I watched the water go down the drain, I told myself that the negative power of the divorce would go down with it. It seemed a powerful image to me and I felt relief.

Celia told me about an experience she had on a three-day raft trip through the Grand Canyon in July. It was very hot, and even though they would bathe in the Colorado River, she yearned for a shower. As part of the trip, the raft stopped at a place where the travelers could climb up a rocky hill into a cave. Inside there was a stream making a waterfall into the cave. The water had been running through the desert and was as hot as a warm shower. Celia told me that standing under that water was the most refreshing experience of her life. Every time she got in a good strong shower after that, she would think of that wonderful waterfall experience. I suggested she take a shower as part of her ceremony. She told me later that in her ceremonial shower, she closed her eyes and let herself remember how wonderful the waterfall had felt and how grateful she was for it. She let all the tension of her day in court flow down the drain with the water. Like the old Roto-Rooter ad said, "And away go troubles down the drain."

CELEBRATIONS

EVEN IF you don't include others in your symbolic ceremony, you may want to have guests afterward. The guests don't have to know you just buried your marriage license, although close friends might even enjoy visiting the grave.

Almost all ceremonies include eating and drinking as a sign of completion. At weddings we have the reception, and funerals usually end with a meal at someone's house.

Eating a meal or special food at the end of a ceremony does two things: It makes the statement that you are committed to enjoying life again, and it reminds you that you are going on with life. You may choose to eat smoked oysters, caviar, or some other delicacy that people save for special occasions. You might drink champagne or sparkling apple cider. The point is to make it special.

Marla felt that an egg was the perfect symbol of a new beginning. She decided to buy an Easter egg decorating kit and decorate eggs she would eat as part of her celebration. She decorated a dozen to represent the 12 years of her marriage, and ate two of them to symbolize the last two years of her marriage that were the most depressing.

Dave felt that being in nature was a great way to celebrate and express his new beginning. He took his three kids and a drive-through family meal to a park and had a picnic as part of his celebration.

Some people want to be around family to celebrate, some prefer being alone, and many prefer a party. Jo had always loved entertaining. Dinner parties were an integral part of her life. She decided to invite several of her women friends over for a party. Most did not realize the evening of the party was the night her divorce was final.

Helen felt that baking bread was almost a sacred experience. To her, bread was a symbol of life. The night she finished her ceremony, she made a special loaf of bread, listening to music as the bread rose. When she ate it, she felt renewed.

There are many ways to celebrate. Some divorcing people choose to take a trip for their celebration. Eating on a cruise ship is a pretty nice way to celebrate the end of your ceremony—particularly if you just threw your rock in the Caribbean.

PASSAGES IN DIVORCE

A DIVORCE doesn't happen overnight. Several steps are involved, and each one of them is worthy of its own ritual: separation, filing for divorce, day in court, the day your divorce is final, subsequent anniversaries, and your ex's remarriage, and the birth of a child who is not yours.

It is possible that these events will come and go without affecting you much, but I think it is good to be prepared. I remember reading about a study in a book on post-surgery physical pain that supports the emotional pain ideas I have. The researchers studied three groups of people comparing their pre-surgery anticipation and the post-surgery recovery. The people who thought it would be a piece of cake had the worst time after the surgery. The second worst recovery occurred for the people who thought they would feel horrible after surgery. The most quickly recovered group were the patients who had moderate expectations for their recovery after surgery. The same is true for divorce—a spousectomy. People who expect their divorce to be nothing often suffer greatly from the pain.

I must admit I was one of those minimizing people after my first divorce. I thought, because of the years of therapy we had been through and the fact that we were not in conflict over the divorce, it would be a piece of cake. I was very shocked when I found myself crying even five years after the divorce. Holidays were the worst. The amount of discomfort I suffered in recovery motivated me to carefully study what helped people recover more quickly, so that neither my clients nor I would suffer to the same level. I hope these ceremonies, and the knowledge that even if you wanted the divorce, it will still hurt, has given you realistic expectations.

Of course, I do not want you to become an emotional hypochondriac and assume that you will suffer. There is a balance to be achieved between anticipating and creating suffering by anticipation and ignoring pain until it sneaks up and gets you. I hope you find a comfortable in-between spot.

Separation

The first step in divorce is separation—one spouse moves out. Just separating and removing your belongings is itself a ritual, but usually that is not enough to help you feel closure. For example, Rachel was devastated to learn that her husband of 12 years had taken his things and moved in with another woman. What bothered her the most was the idea of all the lying that had to occur in order for him to have developed a relationship where he could suddenly be living with someone else. She said, "As I walk through each room of our home, I feel the deception that must have occurred there. I asked him repeatedly in the last three months if there was someone else, and he told me there wasn't. I feel like something evil is hanging in the air."

I suggested she use a Native American ritual to purify her home—burning sage to clear the area of evil spirits. I suggested that she buy a sage smudge (which can be purchased at an incense store) and a feather. She spread the sage smoke into every corner of the house, using the feather to direct the smoke. As she burned the sage, she prayed God's love and the love she and her two sons had for one another would fill that room. She later told me she was sure she could not have tolerated being in that house much longer without feeling she had removed the evil.

Sorting out and separating your physical belongings is another ritual that symbolizes the separation of your two lives. It is difficult to move on until this process occurs. In my case, it took my ex almost a year to remove his things from my house. Having this visual symbol of his things in a pile was a daily reminder of the incompleteness of the divorce, to say nothing of additional clutter to deal with.

The symbol of having your things and your ex's no longer together lets you know exactly what you have to deal with—whose car belongs to whom, which household items are yours, and what you will need to replace. It is difficult to live with much of this unsettled for very long. From a practical point of view, you know what you need to set up your own separate housekeeping when you know what you have left.

Having the other person's stuff out of your space also symbolizes the fact that it is now truly over, which may be why people sometimes avoid the process. Once your belongings are no longer commingled, it symbolizes that your lives are no longer commingled either. When my mother had a series of strokes and went into a nursing home for nine years before her death, it took me seven years to go through her belongings. I kept hoping she would revive enough to enjoy her things again. When you send clothes to a charity organization and start using someone else's things, it means that they are not going to use the items again. Once belongings are removed, used as your own, or disposed of, closure can be complete.

Changing the locks is another way of stating that the separation is permanent. Jenny had repeatedly asked Roger to return his key, but he continued to keep it and came into the house as though it were still his, particularly when she was at work. She felt violated when she came home and found that Roger had been there and removed something without consulting her. Jenny finally changed the locks and took the time to bless her new key.

Filing for Divorce

Separations can go on for years. Finally, however, one partner begins to find the indecision too painful and takes the legal step to file for divorce. This is a perfect time for a ritual.

Marriage tends to create a massive amount of material, which we can use in a ritual of separation. Sarah and

Josh had written the vows for their wedding. When Josh moved in with another woman, Sarah's therapist suggested that she rate how each partner had done at keeping their marriage vows. Josh had vowed to love her and be faithful forever. But he had moved out in September and had been living with his new partner for over five months—that did not help his score on the vows. When he had still not moved back home by Christmas, Sarah decided it was unlikely he would change his mind. She decided those vows would be a good thing to burn on the day she filed for divorce.

The night she filed, Sarah spent some time alone with her thoughts and did a ritual about the pending divorce. She took the vows that they had composed for their marriage and burned them in the fireplace. Sarah followed this with a time of prayer for courage and perseverance over the next few months. The ceremony helped her find strength for all the work of divorcing that lay ahead of her.

Day in Court

Procedures vary from state to state as to when you officially get a divorce. In Nebraska, where I divorced, you do not usually go to court for a temporary settlement unless the parties cannot agree on temporary support. Normally, you go to court for a single hearing, which—if the former partners can agree on the terms of the settlement—can be handled without both parties present. Six months later, if no one has intervened, the divorce becomes final with no further court involvement. Your state may do things differently, so take these concepts and apply them in the way that best fits your particular legal parameters.

Going to court can be very dissatisfying as a ritual experience. When I went to court for my first divorce, we were in and out of there in less than five minutes. My soon-to-be ex-husband sat in the audience. The second time, my soon-to-be ex did not even show up. The judge and I chatted amiably, joking about my radio show. Neither of these events seemed in any way a proper ending to a marriage. Shouldn't there be some form of wailing and gnashing of teeth? This is a devastation that will permanently alter your destiny. No-fault divorces have made these events so brief. However, I would not want to see us go back to expensive battles just to allow a more emphatic ending.

Rick knew he would have to do something more significant to mark his divorce than the quick in-and-out of court. He made a copy of his marriage license and cut it into 20 rectangles to represent the years he and Beth had been married. He arranged those years to represent where they had been living. There were two college years together, three years in the military, ten years in the Midwest, and the last five years on the West Coast. The night he went to court, he sat in front of the fireplace and considered each year they had been together. He would think about the events of each year, as best as he could remember, and then burn the paper that represented that year. He told himself that, as the smoke rose, his grief over the year would go up in the smoke too. He followed the burning of the license by going out to dinner with friends. This did not completely short-circuit the grief of losing his marriage, but it did give him some way to deal with his loss.

When Your Divorce Is Final

People may rally around you when you file and first go to court, but the day the divorce is final may go unnoticed by your friends and family. You may need to create a ceremony. That is exactly what Leslie did.

Leslie looked through the apartment for something that would symbolize the conflict and the pain of the last two years. As she searched, she came across a receipt from the casino her husband frequented. Gambling had been a big factor in her decision to let the marriage go. She decided to combine the receipt with a wedding picture she had treasured. Since she did not have a good place to burn these items, she decided to take them to a nearby creek and tear them into little pieces and let them float away. (I hope these ceremony suggestions won't lead to an increase in water pollution or littering from people dashing to streams and rivers with their mementos!) As she watched the fragments of the receipt and the picture mingle in the water and disappear, she felt that she was letting go of the frustration and pain she had experienced, not only in getting to the divorce, but in having to fight about the few household things they had shared. As Leslie sat by the creek, she thought of the changes in seasons and invited the nature around her to support her in the new season she was beginning.

I have a good friend who married the same violent man twice. He had stabbed her and spent time in jail before they went through their first divorce. After the divorce he had therapy and pronounced himself cured. She married him again. When he abused her again, she divorced him a second time. She needed to do something that would symbolize her vow never to let this marriage rise from the dead again. Around that time she was having a concrete patio poured on her side yard. She made a deal with the contractor to call her just before he poured the tons of concrete in her yard. When he called, she rushed home and put her marriage license on the ground where it would be buried under tons of concrete, never to rise again. It has been seven years since that event. The relationship stayed buried this time.

Anniversaries

Your first wedding anniversary after the divorce might be a little tough. How much this upsets you depends upon how big a deal you made over anniversaries.

For 20 years Bob and Sherry had always eaten lobster on their anniversary. Now Sherry was living with Frank, and Bob was feeling particularly miserable. I joked with him that it was too bad he did not live on the coast, where he could set a lobster free as a symbol of letting go. Since that was not a possibility, I suggested that Bob write Sherry a letter, burn it, and dispose of the ashes in the nearby Missouri River, which eventually empties into the sea. As Bob watched the ashes of his letter float away on his anniversary, he read another letter, which he had written to himself. It reminded him that he needed to be in charge of his own happiness. He then went out with a friend—for a seafood dinner, naturally.

Your Ex's Remarriage and the Birth of Their Child

Some transitions will seal the divorce for you in a very final way: The marriage of your former spouse to someone else, and the birth of their child. Knowing ahead of time how these events may affect you is in itself a way of managing your response.

Gerri had been divorced for three years when she learned through the children that her former husband would be marrying a coworker the following month. She had attended a seminar I had given on divorce, and knew about the idea of ceremonies for these transitions. She prepared for the event in three ways. She selected a poem he had given to her in a Valentine's Day card, and decided to dispose of it. She then chose a poem about strength and courage, which she would read the evening of his wedding. Finally, since her children would be involved in the wedding, she knew she would be alone that evening. She decided to have a small party with her friends who reminded her of the pleasures and satisfactions of her new life. The afternoon of the wedding she flushed the scraps of her husband's poem down the toilet and spent a few minutes reading her poem and praying. She finished off the day preparing for and enjoying the party she had planned.

When your ex-spouse has a child with someone else, it cuts off all hope he or she will ever return—if you had a remnant of hope. Prepare for that event in the same way you would all the other transitions we have mentioned.

The night Don's ex-wife, Ann, remarried, he had gotten very drunk and then spent the next day in bed with a hangover. Now Ann was about to have a baby with her new husband, and he knew he had to do better this time. Don did not have any mementos of the marriage left, so he wrote a letter to his ex-wife telling her he was still angry at her for giving up on him, but that he had to let go of that anger now. He knew this baby's birth represented the final end to his hopes that she would return. He decided that when he heard the baby was born, he would throw the letter in a trash can at the nearby park where he and Ann had often gone for picnics. He was going to carry the letter in his pocket until then. Because he had planned for the event, Don handled the news of the baby's birth better than he would have done otherwise, and a lot better than he managed Ann's new marriage.

WHAT'S LEFT?

CEREMONIES MAY reveal what is still unfinished for you. Sometimes the event for which you are doing the ceremony, such as the day the divorce is final, may not move you that much, but the ceremony lets you know that something else is unfinished.

A year after my second divorce, I was searching for an object I could bury as a symbol of the end of the marriage. I came across something we had made for us on a trip to China. It was a "chop" that represented the title to our book on marriage. A chop is a seal, like a logo or signature. You may have seen these red stamps on the bottom of Chinese prints. I felt that the chop symbolized the marriage pretty well. As I made the hole in the yard, buried the chop, and made a little cross for the grave, I noticed I did not feel much about the marriage and the divorce. But when I did the latter part of the ceremony, which was to sing hymns, I felt there was a lot of energy there—my relationship with God was where my conflicts lay. I felt peace with the ending of the marriage, but confused about God's change of plans for me.

My use of rituals to move my feelings along is legend with my older children. When my second husband moved out, I burned letter, papers, and pictures. Our fireplace had been the location of frequent ceremonies. When my daughter and her husband came for a visit, she noticed that many of my ex's things were still either in our bedroom or next to it. She offered to box them up and get them away from my immediate space. When she had all the stuff at the top of the stairs, she asked, "Where shall we put this? The fireplace?" I laughed and said, "No. I think we are stuck preserving it in the basement."

Ceremonies can help give you closure, ease the pain, and help you know when the emotions are over. When you look at a picture that you are about to burn and notice that the sight of the two of you together has little energy for you, that is a sign you have completed the divorce. Heal and learn from the ceremonies you create to take you through the stages of your transition to a satisfying single life.

Key Points About Rituals

Times of transition are made more smooth by a ritual to mark the passage. Passages in divorce are: separation, filing for divorce, day in court, the day your divorce is final, subsequent anniversaries, your ex's remarriage, and the birth of a child who is not yours.

DESIGN YOUR RITUAL:
- Identify the purpose of the ritual and what is still unfinished for you
- Prepare for the ritual by deciding what symbols you will use, when you will do the ritual, who else will be included, what you will wear, where you will perform the ritual, and what you need to do to get ready emotionally and psychologically to do the ritual

(continued)

Key Points About Rituals–continued

- Include a vow of commitment to yourself
- Perform the ceremony
- Make a transition from the ritual back into your everyday life
- Celebrate the completion of the ritual and your determination to move on

CHAPTER FOUR

The Great Escape

*Sixty minutes of thinking of any kind
is bound to lead to confusion and unhappiness.*
—JAMES THURBER

HOW DID psychotherapy and our culture get the idea that everything must be "worked through"? Like a sprained muscle, maybe some things should be left alone to heal. I have already made it clear that you have to put in some mental time understanding as best you can what led to the ending of the marriage. But it doesn't seem to me that you have to stay stuck there for seven or eight years.

Commonly, therapists advise newly divorced people not to get seriously involved for two years. Making a good choice of mate when you are fresh out of one marriage is unlikely for three reasons: You will likely choose based on how opposite the new mate is from the old; avoidance of the pain of the divorce is futile and clouds your best judgment; and you have robbed yourself of the opportunity to get reacquainted with yourself that being single can bring.

After 16 years of marriage, I leapt into an unfortunate second marriage with a partner who had "issues," as they say in the therapy world. When I got out of that second marriage, which lasted 10 years, I realized I had never had the time yet in my life to ask, "What do I like? What do I want? Who am I?" I had been such a chameleon in my marriages. If my husband liked golf, I played golf. If he liked traveling, I traveled. If he liked to eat pizza, we went to a pizza parlor. I never had stopped to find out what I wanted, who I was outside of my work, and what was good for me. To avoid getting involved in another relationship too quickly and losing yourself in the process, you can use healthy escapes.

Step four is the fun step: Temporarily getting away from the divorce through fantasy escapes such as movies, music, or writing; physical escapes through bodily comforts; profitable escapes by throwing yourself into work; and true vacations. Healthy escapes are alternatives to endless pity parties. Unhealthy escapes involve drinking, gambling, repeated empty social flings, compulsive shopping, and lack of attention to the details of life—such as paying your bills. These will get you into trouble eventually. Healthy escapes serve two functions: To give you a break from the painful transitions of divorce, and to help you have enough fun by yourself that you do not rush back into a relationship.

FANTASY

DO YOU enjoy reading novels? If so, you have a big jump on this method. Fantasy is defined as imagination or the product of imagination. Being able to get into your own fantasy or someone else's is a great way to escape when you are going through a troubling time.

Even though I advocate keeping your awareness in the present, I am about to tell you to live in your imagination to escape an unpleasant situation. The sense of balance and choice seems the key to whether this is healthy or not. If you have a car accident because you are fantasizing about your dream lover of the future, or if you're reading your favorite spy novel and miss an important business meeting, then you are too far into fantasy. But if you say to yourself, "This is not the most fun time in my life, so I will use my mind to play in the present," then you're on the track I am suggesting.

There are two ways to escape into healthy fantasy. One is using the fantasies that others create for you, such as movies, books, and music. The other is creating fantasies for yourself.

Movies

Felicia told me that since her divorce she had become a movie addict. She and her 10-year-old went to the local video store every Tuesday night and rented movies. I told her, "Go for it!" When you are absorbed in a good movie, you can forget the loneliness, forget the bills, forget the overwhelming nature of single parenting, and escape for an hour or two. If it is funny, that is even better.

Books

My roommate from college lived her life in rural Kansas. When she divorced she read herself healthy! She read nearly every volume in the Hutchinson Public Library. Books are a wonderful way to feel less lonely, whether they are novels or nonfiction. I often find that when I read something I enjoy, I feel like the writer is a friend of mine. I love to read mystery and suspense novels. A "good read" is a great escape. Going through divorce was when I most needed to lose myself in my fiction, which I often did.

Music

Listening to music can be a deeply comforting, spirit-altering escape. There is music for all occasions. If you need to feel energized (rock), soothed (jazz, chamber music), inspired (all forms), or even organized (Bach), there is music you can escape into.

My son Nick, who is a successful musician, was initially surprised when young people came up to him and said, "Your music changed my life, man." The more he was aware of the effect of his lyrics, the more he tried to include uplifting messages in his music. On his album, "311," which came out during my divorce, were the lyrics, "You have to trust your instincts and let go of regrets. You have to bet on yourself. Now start, 'cause you're the best bet." As I would drive to work, I would listen to those lyrics and feel inspired to make it through another day.

Both my adult sons are musicians. My jazz son, Zack, once said to me, "Music is so wonderful. If you are unhappy, you can play. If you are joyful, you can play. If you are bored, you can play. Whatever you need, music can be that for you." (If you have a child taking music lessons, now would be a good time to encourage them to practice.) If you can play an instrument, do.

As I went through my divorce, I would play the piano and make up little songs about what had happened or might happen in the future. I am not sufficiently knowledgeable to write these down well, but making them up was a good escape.

Writing

Writing is a great antidote for loneliness. When I am writing, I picture the people who may read my books. Even if you don't think you could ever write anything publishable, maybe you could think of writing your family history for your grandchildren, letters to a spiritual influence, or a fairy tale for a child. Now that I am an author, people often say, "I've always thought I have a book in me." This might be a great time to let that come out.

Letter writing is a great escape. An Australian actress interviewed on the radio talked about writing to an American pen pal in her teens after her father had died. Later, when the actress moved to the United States, she and her pen pal became adult friends. The loss of her father may have made the letter-writing an even more important escape.

Maybe you could make up stories to escape into during this transition. Why not? I mentioned earlier that Sue Grafton, an enormously successful mystery writer, got her

start after her husband had left her for another woman—
she wanted to plan the perfect murder. What about writing
a story about the perfect romance? Or writing a fairy tale
with yourself as a hero? You never know, it might become
fantasy for profit!

Sara had a more serious side to her fantasy. She had
been depressed and had thought about suicide. I felt it
unlikely that she was actually going to act on those
thoughts. I asked her to write a story of her funeral and
how people who loved her felt afterward. This was not a
happy fantasy, but it was good use of her imagination.
Creating that story allowed her to get perspective on how
much people would miss her, be hurt, and even angry at
her for leaving them.

I wrote letters to my fantasized next-husband for a
while. That helped me clarify exactly what it was that I
wanted in my future. In some ways, it was the best of
both worlds: someone to talk to, but no real person to actually have to negotiate with on a daily basis. What a
good deal!

Art

If you are fortunate enough to be able to draw, sculpt, or
paint, this would be a good time to throw yourself into an
art project. Vickie had been painting as a hobby for a
long time, but during her marriage she was never able to
spend as much time painting as she would have liked.
She decided that her divorce had given her the gift of
time to take her art more seriously. She found she had a

new depth to her work that came out of her painful growth experiences in divorce, and escaping into her painting enabled her to develop an impressive portfolio.

Todd had a degree in art and was working in computer graphics when his marriage ended. He decided that one of the first things he would do in his new home was sculpt his frustration about the divorce. He escaped into the work, enjoying the physical nature of sculpture and enjoying his freedom from the keyboard and mouse. His finished sculpture expressed his newfound feelings.

Your art may be more of a craft. Marissa decided that she would make presents for her extended family now that she was not filling her life up with her husband. She escaped for a few months into making quilts for her sisters' families for Christmas.

If you don't consider yourself an artist, this may be your opportunity to learn more about it. When I was married, I never had time to visit museums. I had been interested in art and art history as a student, but life had swept me along—and Omaha did not offer many exhibitions. When I moved to the Dallas–Fort Worth area, I joined both the major museums (Kimball and the Dallas Museum of Art) and attended a function or an exhibit once a month. Opening yourself to creativity, whether it is yours or someone else's, is healing.

Your mind is a potential playground. As long as you know you are playing, you are developing the creative side of you, having fun, often indirectly dealing with your feelings, and healing at the same time.

VACATIONS

MARCIA DECIDED that she would take a vacation from her divorce one day every week. While she was away from home, she would pretend that she was not a single parent; she would say, "Stop!" to herself if she started to think about the divorce; and she would not do anything about the legal process that day. While not thinking about the divorce was difficult (particularly since others at work had yet to learn that Tuesdays were no-divorce days), she did improve her ability to control her thinking by taking her vacation from divorce.

When Jeff divorced, he decided to go on a trip that he had always wanted to take. For years he had been a member of an ecologically minded group that would, for a fairly substantial fee, allow you to participate in an archeological dig, record observations of animals or plants, or be a part of some other kind of scientific study. He participated in a Native American archeological dig in another state and met all sorts of interesting people. His decision to go on this kind of absorbing vacation helped him feel useful. It also helped him forget about the divorce temporarily.

Movies and stories often portray the adventures of people who take the opportunity to be very different when they go on vacation, as though they take a vacation from their personalities while away from their homes. Lydia decided she was going to break out of her middle-age slump and begin to loosen up now that her husband was gone. She bought a more colorful wardrobe, had a makeover, lost 10 pounds, and got a new hair color and style. Then she went on a cruise with her college alumni group to try out the new Lydia. Having made some changes, she felt more confident and therefore attracted more people. In some ways, taking a permanent vacation from the old you may be something that you wish to do as part of your divorce. Going on a vacation may be a good start.

The first year I was divorced, I went on a vacation with my sons to Club Med in Mexico. There I did all sorts of things I either had never done or had not done in nearly 20 years. I danced for hours. I sailed. I played golf again for the first time in many years. I enjoyed flirting. My only regret was that I did not have the courage to learn to use the circus trapeze—but even writing about it makes my palms sweat. The vacation reminded me of what I could do now that I was in charge of my own life. I could go anywhere, live anywhere, eat anything I wanted, and dress to my own taste. It was all up to me to create the lifestyle I wanted.

Sherry had been married for 15 years. Although she was in her forties, she looked much younger. Like most women who have been married for a while, she did not know if men found her attractive or not. (Most of us don't test that question too vigorously while we are married—it makes a spouse nervous.) When her divorce was final, she took her son and daughter on a cruise and met several single men. Their response reassured her that she was still able to attract men. It would be great if we didn't need the responses of others, but there are not many other ways to reassure yourself that you are sexually appealing. Fortunately, a smile or a look is often enough to know you are wanted without having to do anything about it.

A vacation back to your childhood home can not only be a good escape, it can be a centering experience—particularly if you have friends and relatives there who appreciate you. When her husband moved out, Dottie went back to her home in Pennsylvania to visit. Walking the streets where she had played as a child, seeing old friends from high school, and visiting relatives reminded her she was a valuable person and she had been a happy child with great potential for a good life. Being there gave her the determination that she would not let this setback be more than a glitch. Escaping back home gave her a new perspective on herself and her strength.

Vacations are escapes *from* something—divorce, the legal hostilities, or the daily experience of loneliness or drudgery. They are also escapes *to* something: new adventures, new ways of being, and new possibilities. Although it is important not to get yourself in debt when you are going through the financial devastation of divorce, even a day trip can be a great change. I love long car trips because I can listen to tapes and think for hours without any interruptions.

BODILY PLEASURES

IT CAN be a shock to the system to go from being physically intimate with someone—even if the sex wasn't all that great at the end—to not being touched at all. Research shows that massage and exercise have great benefit in helping you handle stress, and this divorce might be the most stressful event of your life.

I was very fortunate when I was going through divorce because I could afford to have a massage once a week. (An inexpensive way to do this is to go to a massage school to be a guinea pig for budding massage therapists.) Being thoroughly touched once a week was comforting, relaxing, and a great escape from all the upset going on in and around me.

I know you have heard this before, but exercise is a great escape. Chuck said that he doesn't know how he would have made it through his divorce if he had not been a runner. He would go out for a run feeling that his insides were so tight that he might implode. At the end of a 45-minute run, he would feel like all his nerves were lined up in an orderly fashion.

Swimming, an exercise much easier on the knees, was my escape. Three times a week during my divorce, I would swim laps for a half an hour. True, my goggles would often fill with tears, but no one can tell where the water is coming from when you are swimming. Afterward, I would feel more peaceful even though nothing had changed.

Heat is a also a great thing for stress (spoken as a true Texan!). In my opinion spas and saunas should be part of the regimen for surviving divorce. After a serious baking in a steam room, it is hard to feel too upset. I would tell myself that, as the water left my body, so did all the tension and conflict. Even if you can't afford the spa, a hot bath is available to most everyone. Pamper yourself by scenting the water with a relaxing lavender oil bead or other scent, and make it your time away from worry.

BEING WITH OTHERS

SO FAR we have explored physically escaping—as in vacations, escaping through fantasies, and escaping by doing physical interventions with the body. But you can also escape your divorce worries by being with other people.

Brenda told me that her therapist, like many therapists, advised her not to date for two years after her divorce. My first question was "Has your therapist ever been divorced?" Two years is a long time to go without any company of the opposite sex. There is no reason why you can't go out on dates right after your divorce—as long as you don't make any permanent commitments during this vulnerable time. My limit was usually three dates. At that point, the other person would either begin to expect sex or begin to talk of a more exclusive dating commitment, which I was sure I was not ready for right after the divorce. This is not to say I never went out with someone longer than three dates, but three dates did seem to be my pattern.

I have escaped with both feet into the keep-yourself-busy-with-groups-and-friends scene. I usually have more opportunities than I can take advantage of in any one weekend because I have friends and belong to singles' groups. When I am not dating, this is great.

Admittedly, it is much easier to be divorced in a big city. I am very lucky that I live in a city where there are over 30 large singles' groups. In the Dallas–Fort Worth area, I can go to a singles' group that builds homes for Habitat for Humanity, a singles' group for people who love to sail, numerous dances, religiously affiliated groups, and so on. My city is singles' heaven. But even if you live in a less-populated area, there are often singles' newspapers with pages of personals.

I find there are two types of singles' groups. The first is the type where there is a dance and you feel lots of pressure to meet someone that night and make plans. The second is what I think of as a pseudo-family, where people get to know each other in a variety of settings, discussion groups, parties, or outings. Of course, I like those better. I am not sure that these singles' groups are necessarily the greatest places to meet people to date, but they are great for having some fun things to do on a weekend. The long-standing group with a family atmosphere is a mixed blessing if you are new. When you walk in for the first time and most of the jokes are in-jokes, it can make you feel like an outsider. In the sailing club I recently joined, the group all went to the Caribbean together last year. It will take a long time to overcome being a non-Caribbean-trip member.

Other ways to meet new people include dating services, ads, and the Internet. Video dating services are expensive, but may be worth it when you want to get married. I would wait for a couple of years to fork out that kind of money. There are cheaper ways to meet people, including personal ads in the local paper, but be very cautious about where you meet the person, for your safety's sake. I have met a few good men through personal ads. There are matching services on the Internet, and I have experimented with these with a small amount of success. By "success" I mean meeting someone to go out with at least two times.

In many areas, particularly less populated areas, churches offer opportunities to belong to groups. Usually, at least one church will cater to the singles crowd. When there are over 100 people in a single-adult class, you know that you are going to meet people doing the same things you are doing.

Singles groups may be great for meeting friends of the same sex as well as someone to date. Why do you need single friends when you are divorced? First, because they will be looking for social times when you are. I have a favorite woman friend, Jody, who is also a single parent. I spend at least one evening a weekend with her. She is an English teacher interested in the same cultural events I am and dealing with many of the frustrations I deal with as a single mom. We validate each other's experiences and, since she has a great since of humor, we often can lighten each other's spirits. When some weekends are over we look at each other and say, "Okay, now we have two more things for the not-to-do-in-Dallas list."

If you need plenty of alone time, you may find groups draining. Still, I do not know any better way to join a community or a segment of the community than to meet people in groups. You may quickly develop a small set of friends and then avoid groups, if that is your style. That's fine, but you need to keep from being too isolated when you are going through a divorce.

PROFITABLE ESCAPING

HARD WORK is something our culture rewards. Since it has financial benefits, you might want to escape into your career, particularly if you love what you do. The secret, again, is having some balance between work and home life.

Mary was a therapist. When she went through her divorce she felt that she would have gone crazy without her work. Being able to throw herself into other people's problems was therapeutic for her. When she was in a session with a client, she found it easy to think about the client and not to think about her divorce. Naturally, she made more money during this time because she saw so many clients—and that provided her other comforts as well.

You can make a career shift after a divorce, but give it a year before doing anything too drastic. It is hard to make great decisions when so much has changed and you are hurting. If you give yourself some healing time, it will improve your decision making. You might want to make a small change in how you work. Although Jim was a lawyer in private practice, he did not have enough clients to keep him busy. He decided to work half-time for Legal Aid to keep himself occupied. Seeing people in desperate circumstances helped him cope with his loss.

Jack's job as a telephone repairman had become automatic for him. It was not enough to take his mind off his divorce. Even so, he put in as much overtime as he could so he could make more money for things he could enjoy, such as buying a new fishing boat.

SERVICE

A JOB may provide the opportunity to escape in a well-rewarded way, but helping others as a volunteer may help you too. A woman who works in the hospice movement told me that if you really want to figure out what life is all about, work with the dying. Now that might be too stressful for you, but working with the illiterate, the poor, the young—all those fellow humans who are suffering in their own ways—keeps things in perspective and gives you a chance to feel good about what you are doing. Deepak Chopra says that if you want to be successful, ask, "How can I help?" Look around in your community. Ask that question yourself and see how you can contribute.

Gerry was a teacher near retirement when her husband left. She decided to devote her free time to the literacy program. When her husband left, it felt like he didn't need her any more. The people she worked with in the literacy program felt they needed her very much. These were adults who were embarrassed and limited by not being able to read. In many ways, she felt more important than she had for a long time as a teacher.

THE SOONER THE BETTER

YOU CANNOT truly run away from your suffering in a divorce, but you can keep it from being the central focus of your every minute. When I work with alcoholics trying to maintain sobriety, I ask them, "What are you going to do to fill your life up now that alcohol is out?" Drinking used to be the center of everything. They need to do some major reconstruction of their lives to find a new focus. In the same way, divorcing people have to find new ways to fill up their lives away from their marriages. Playing is working on healing, whether the recovery is from alcoholism or divorce. Make a conscious effort to create healthy escapes and you will feel better sooner.

It's OK to Escape

Avoid the idea that you must keep dealing with your pain full-time. Remember that whatever you focus upon tends to expand. Make plans for fun.

FANTASY:
- Created by others: movies, novels, music
- Created by you: novels, music, poems, letters to someone in the future

VACATIONS:
- Set aside time to not think or do anything about the divorce
- Take a real vacation
- Take a vacation from your old personality

BODILY PLEASURES:
- Get a massage
- Get some exercise
- Raise your body temperature in a hot bath or sauna

SOCIAL LIFE WITH NO COMMITMENTS:
- Singles groups: meat market/surrogate family
- Dating services, Internet, and personals
- Church groups

(continued)

It's OK to Escape–continued

ESCAPING FOR PROFIT (WORK):
- Gear up your career
- Consider a career change

SERVICE TO OTHERS:
- Ask, "How can I help?"
- Volunteer to help others who are in tough situations

CHAPTER FIVE

The Mental Tune-Up

Happiness is beneficial for the body,
but it is grief that develops the powers of the mind.

—MARCEL PROUST

I N CHAPTER ONE we looked at the necessity of finding a way to understand the loss of love. In this chapter we are again going to explore the story-generating quality of the mind.

Earlier, I implied a distrust of this story-generating quality of the brain, suggesting that the stories you create about your divorce may or may not be accurate. Again, we are going to consider how the mind works and this time we are going to consciously take charge of it.

Rather than allowing thoughts to float through our minds, we can make choices about what we are thinking and create thinking habits that will speed and increase our healing. We do have power over our thoughts and power to deliberately put ideas into our minds. In the world of computers, scientists point out that what comes out of the computer is determined by what you put into it. They call it GIGO—garbage in, garbage out. Combat the GIGO syndrome in yourself by making sure that what you are putting into your mind is healing rather than destructive.

We will look at four ways to work with the nature of our minds to speed the healing process and discover

more peace: oppositional thinking, other-focused thinking, gainful thinking, and silencing the mind.

OPPOSITIONAL THINKING

DO YOU ever feel like your sadness or your anger is almost a monster pushing you around? As you go through
divorce, you may be waking up in the morning to a mental punch in the face as you remember that your mate is
gone and you are going to face another lonely day. You
might find yourself doing and saying things that aren't at
all like you, like bad-mouthing your ex in front of the
children or having sex with people you don't really care
about. If so, you need to learn oppositional thinking: resisting the unhelpful thoughts that come to your mind.

Name Your Demon

People often feel bullied by their misery in a divorce. I
like to think of this negativity as a bully or a demon
pushing around our emotions. Which of your emotions
seems most out of control? Is it your anger? Is it your
sadness? Then give those feelings a name that reflects
how your feelings are keeping you trapped, keeping you
from acting in your best interests, or encouraging you to
do things you later regret. Perhaps you could call it the
Divorce Demon or the Anger Bully. If you are having
trouble deciding what your demon is, observe your

thoughts and actions for a day and see what comes up most frequently.

Beth was lonely and sad after her husband left, but every time she started to reach for the phone to call someone, her demon would whisper in her ear, "Why bother your friends with your misery? You'd just bring them down too. Why splash all your grief and anger on everyone else?" Most of the time the demon would win, and Beth would not pick up the phone. I encouraged Beth to develop her oppositional thinking plan. First, she labeled her demon the Isolation Demon, because it prevented her from reaching out to others. Second, she began to notice what she did naturally to resist her isolating ideas and did more of those things. For example, she would stand up to her demon by saying, "I have been there for my friends; now it is their turn. I deserve to be loved and comforted by my friends." Ultimately, she said to her Demon, "Don't you tell me what to do! I'll call anybody I want to any time I want to!" That was good oppositional thinking. Her shift from passively accepting her thoughts to challenging them was an important step in resisting the isolation of her divorce.

My son Nick was dealing with the breakup of a two-year relationship. He put a sign on his bedroom door that said, "Soul-Suckers must be circumnavigated." You might think of your divorce demon as the Soul-Sucker, since it could be draining you.

Once you have picked your demon's name, you can begin to be aware of how it is sabotaging your recovery from the divorce. Ask yourself some questions: "How does my Divorce Demon push me around? Does it make me miserable by going over and over scenes where I felt betrayed or where I acted in a way I am ashamed of now?" "Does the Abandonment Demon convince me that I am not lovable or desirable?" By consciously separating yourself from your thoughts, you provide yourself a tool for being more objective and less self-sabotaging than you might otherwise be.

Stand Up to Your Bully

Skip was very angry at his wife for taking his two middle-school-aged boys and leaving him. Because he was so angry, he would talk to anyone and everyone about how awful she was and how unfair it was that she left. He became even angrier when he discovered that she had had another relationship for several months before the breakup, with a man who had much more money than Skip. People in general are uncomfortable with anger, and this was getting old fast. His friends started to avoid him. His sons did not want to be around him because he would try to get them to agree that his ex was evil for leaving. His Anger Bully was costing him dearly. He came to me in desperation, in danger of losing everyone he loved.

When it came to his friends, we decided, Skip needed to stop letting the bully convince him that he was going to get justice by getting others on his side. I asked him to keep track of all the times he stood up to the Anger Bully and resisted bad-mouthing his ex. His main strategy for resisting the bully was to think of what it was costing him—his children's respect and the enjoyment of times with his friends. He was able to attract more friends once his venomous anger was not present in most of his interactions. He was not wrong for being angry. Anger is part of the package when you feel betrayed. However, talking about it to your children and spending most of your time talking about it to your friends will wear out your welcome.

The desire for justice often motivates us to persist in being pushed around by our demons. Justice is rarely available in divorce, particularly since no-fault divorce is the law in most states. Women who devote years to being homemakers and putting their husbands' and children's interests first often become pushed around by the Injustice Bully. But it is a waste of time to kick ourselves for being suckers. The only reasonable option is to stand up to that bully by saying, "Look, I did the best I knew how at the time. I was the kind of generous person I wanted to be." Then resist time-wasting regrets or rehashing what a sucker you were for putting yourself last. Many people are as angry at themselves for allowing the injustice to happen in the marriage as they are for the injustice inflicted upon them by divorce.

The demons of divorce are usually irrational, impractical, or exaggerated. The best tool for standing up to them is to be as rational as possible. Sure we all wish that we could have justice, be loved and forgiven, and be appreciated for all our good intentions, but it is irrational to expect that in life. Your parents may have told you, "Life isn't always fair," and they were right. Talking to yourself in emotion-laden terms is a way to suffer much longer than you would have to otherwise.

My friend Tanya devoted most of her life to raising her five children. When her husband, Steve, left her for a much younger, thinner woman, she was furious. Tanya would get angry all over again when she would hear that Steve had joined the country club, or that Steve had taken his new wife and his new son on a Caribbean vacation. She realized she was allowing the Injustice Bully to injure her by getting her angry over and over. She stood up to her demon by refusing to let her ex ruin her present life by making her dwell on what he was enjoying. She focused on all the joys she had with her children and how much closer they were to her than to her ex. Above all, she would treat her thoughts about injustice as something that was trying to push her around and keep her from enjoying life the way she could.

I asked both Skip and Tanya an important question: "How is your future going to be different from the future your bully has planned for you?" Skip and Tanya both realized that their bullies had planned a lonely, bitter future for them, isolated from enjoyment and, in Skip's case, even from friends and children.

There are many bullies to oppose when you go through divorce. But whether you are dealing with the All-Men-Are-Evil Bully, the Women-Can't-Be-Trusted Bully, the Shyness Bully, or your own special demon, the steps of standing up to it are the same:

1. Think of the bully as something that is outside you and trying to push you around
2. Name your demon
3. Notice how it tricks you and gets you to do things that are not successful for you
4. Notice how you stand up to your bully, and do it more often
5. As you stand up to your bully, notice how it changes your present and your future

I invite you to move more quickly through your divorce by using this technique. I know you will have upset feelings, feelings of injustice and loss, but don't let them turn into a controlling force in your life. Let them pass you like a low-pressure system that is passing through, not making a permanent change in your internal climate. If you experiment with the steps outlined here, you can change how you feel. Other people are counting on you to recover and move on. Thinking of them is other-focused thinking.

OTHER-FOCUSED THINKING

I SOMETIMES kid about how I have not been allowed the luxury of a real depression because my children would not permit it. They won't even allow me an hour's nap! It is as if they have to shake me to be sure I am still breathing as soon as I am still. The idea of spending two or three days in bed being depressed is beyond what I can imagine getting away with as a mom. That is, in the end, a blessing.

After my last divorce, there were plenty of days that I would have stayed in bed with the covers over my head had it not been for Angie, Nick, Zack, and Patrick—my children. I knew that if I gave into my suffering, they would be sucked down with me. They would suffer much more and much longer from the divorce. So on those days that I wanted to stay in bed, I roused myself for them and did whatever there was to do next.

I suspect there have been times you wanted to make a nest in your bedroom and refuse to come out. You may have even indulged yourself in a major pity party. But you owe it to your family, your friends, and perhaps even people you have yet to meet to keep living your life. This is the other-focused thinking that comes into play when you are going through a divorce.

Annie was trying to hole up in her room when her four-year-old daughter, Becca, climbed into her mom's bed. Becca had heard her mother crying and was on the verge of tears herself. Becca said, "Mommy, please don't be sad." Annie told me later, "I knew I couldn't cry in front of her then. It is just too selfish for me to shut down like that. I think it makes Becca afraid that the people she counts on can't handle life."

Children try so hard to take care of their parents, particularly when a relationship breaks up. A successful executive told me that his 10-year-old daughter tried to be a little homemaker for her daddy when he was going through a divorce. As part of her attempts she would do laundry without being asked. Unfortunately, she mistook the pile of suits waiting to go to the dry cleaners as laundry that needed to go into the washer and dryer. Needless to say, they became misshapen doll clothes following their washing.

When I had my daily radio call-in show, I would often get calls from older adults who were under great stress because their adult children were suffering the pain of divorce. You can't stop yourself from hurting when your life is turned upside down, and you need not feel guilty for your feelings. However, you can try to move through your pain in a timely manner—if not for yourself, then for your parents, your children, or your friends. I am not asking you to deny your feelings. I know that you have to set aside time for yourself to allow this enormous change of divorce to sink in. Perhaps that can be during a scheduled "meditation" time or private time, away from the rest of your family. The next time you are thinking of dropping out from those who love and need you, or raging about life, or drinking just a few too many to forget, remember those who care and are counting on you to heal.

GAINFUL THINKING

ONE OF the best suggestions I received in the first three weeks after my second husband left was to make a daily list of the things I now could do because he was gone. The friend who made this suggestion had known us well and seen the limitations of my life with him. She was sure there were some benefits I could notice right away. Of course, the first thing I noticed was that I now had the TV remote control in my hand. I could surf the channels on cable television, lingering as long as I wished on whatever caught my fancy. The second was how much more fun meals were. My soon-to-be ex was a very picky eater. When he left, I discovered the delightful enjoyment of cooking with wine, mushrooms, peppers, and a variety of veggies. This was an important compensation.

What is on your list? Maybe it is being able to watch sports on television uninterrupted. Maybe it is spending money on an outfit without having to be accountable to someone for the cost. I am sure you can find some gains immediately. Even wonderful relationships involve compromises and sacrifices, which you no longer have to make. List your gains.

Amid these small daily gains, you will probably find some very significant ones. What major decision did you put off or skip due to your relationship? Now is your chance to do something important that you have postponed. You could go back to school. You could change careers. You could move to another city, which is what I did. I don't advise making a huge change immediately, in reaction to the divorce, but you can begin thinking about what you might do. That itself is a gain. Now you may be saying, "But, Pat, I'm broke." It takes a few years to recover financially from a divorce, but at least you are now totally in charge of your own financial destiny. Although I had a much lower family income after my divorce, I was delighted to be as frugal as I wanted or as spendthrift as I wanted.

Divorce affects a person's sense of identity, particularly for women who thought of themselves as a "Mrs." A divorce decree is a good time to gain a new identity by a name change, although for the price of legal services, it can happen anytime. I was born with the name Patricia Ann Hudson. Patricia was fine, but I had always thought that Ann was not a very inventive name for the only child of two parents with graduate degrees in English. Ophelia, Penelope, Emily (as in Brontë) might have been more expected. After all, my father had been given the name of a charismatic preacher-poet of his parents' time, Lofton. My mother was named after her grandfather, a ferryman on the Cumberland River, Jesse (spelled Jessie for her). When I had married, I had taken my husband's family name as a middle name and he had taken Hudson as his middle name. But now it was time to pick a new name.

I felt that this choice was going to be an important symbol for my future and what I wanted to remember or gain from this change. Many feminist women I knew had taken their mother's maiden name as their last name when they divorced. I liked that idea of carrying on a female lineage. Still, I wanted something more spiritual or mythical that would symbolize this transition. I decided to find a middle name that began with the letter O. Since my ex-husband's name began with an O, I did not want to change three of my diplomas again—as I had when I married—to say nothing of all those credit cards either. I therefore concentrated on O names.

Onan first came to mind. Although single life was sexually frustrating, I did not want that biblical name to be my symbol. (Onan was the man who spilled his seed on the ground and took heat for it.) But when I looked in conventional books of names, none of the few female O names suggested what I wanted to convey with my name.

During the divorce process, I had gone on some religious retreats and studied the history of pre-Christian religions, particularly the goddess tradition. I decided a goddess name might represent the positive force I wanted to express in my name. I found some names I liked, such as Danu, but I thought I would try to hold out for the big O, unless that became an impossible quest.

It occurred to me that mythology might have something for me. I pulled out my dusty 1979 copy of Bulfinch's *Mythology*. At the back was a wonderful Dictionary and Index section. I found all sorts of names and myths that might suit the occasion. For example, the name Ariadne. She was the daughter of King Minos of Crete who fell in love with Theseus. She had rescued him by giving him a sword and helping him kill the Minotaur and escape the maze. After they escaped, he abandoned her. Her laments inspired Bacchus to marry her and give her a crown which, upon her death, was transformed into a celestial constellation. I related to this story.

In spite of the happy ending to Ariadne's story, I did not want my life to become "a lament," nor did I want to drag around a name that focused on the past instead of my future. Where I was headed was much more important to me than where I had been. My hunt continued through Bulfinch's index until I found a name in the O's—Olwen.

The story came from a Welsh tale that reflected part of my mongrel American blood—I have British, French, Dutch, Scot, Irish, and Cherokee heritage. The love story of Kilwich and Olwen tells of a young man, Kilwich, who announces to his father and stepmother that he wants to take a wife. The stepmother declares that it is Kilwich's destiny to marry Olwen the daughter of Yspadaden Penkawr. As soon as his stepmother makes this declaration, Kilwich knows Olwen must be his wife and feels filled with love for Olwen. His father suggests that Kilwich go to visit their cousin, King Arthur, and ask for his help in finding Olwen.

Kilwich, with the help of King Arthur and a few of Arthur's knights, goes through terrible trials set up by Olwen's father, a king, to become the husband of Olwen. He uses strength, clever strategies, and his befriending nature to succeed.

When Kilwich first sees Olwen, she is wearing a robe of flame-colored silk, with hair golden as the flower of the broom, skin whiter than the foam of the sea. Whoever beheld her was filled with love for her and, due to her goodness, and wherever she stepped, four little flowers sprung up. (Okay. Maybe that is not exactly me—I haven't noticed flowers behind me and I am not a blond and if my skin looks like sea foam it would have to be after a

The Mental Tune-Up

garbage barge accident, but still a worthy name to live up to.)

At a time when I had little energy, I selected a name that would be a symbol for me of what I would require in a relationship. I told myself that every time I wrote or said my name it would be a signal to never settle for less in myself or from another in a relationship, but to hold out for a partner of courage, honor, in harmony with nature, who would be willing to go to great lengths to be with me as Kilwich had done for Olwen. There have been times when that name would jolt me back to what I wanted and help me decide to be appropriately picky in my dating. I used the opportunity to change my name as a chance to gain something new as part of my identity shift from wife to independent woman.

The gains have been enormous on so many levels. I deliberately chose to use the event to radically change my lifestyle. I moved from the Midwest to the South to make certain that I spent the last half of my life in warm weather. I took the opportunity to get more involved in church, from which I had been discouraged during my marriage. I had the pleasure of having more time to devote to my youngest child. I was free to devote time to my aging parents. The divorce rekindled in me the possibility of having a great relationship—although, as of this writing, there is nothing to report. I developed a new circle of friends who were primarily single women. But by far the most important gain was the spiritual gain.

If you have just lost your love, you may not find much comfort in what I am about to write, but you will probably hear it from others besides me: You will grow through this. As one woman I met who was also going through a divorce joked, "I am beginning to think these opportunities for growth might be overrated." However, the truth is that I did grow through my divorce, and perhaps proportionately to the misery from the divorce. The first divorce was not a very miserable experience, and although I grew somewhat, I grew much more from my devastating second divorce. Spiritually, the second divorce made me wrestle with issues of meaning and the purpose of suffering that otherwise I would have blithely ignored. That spiritual journey will be the topic of my next book.

Clearly, looking for what you are and will be gaining from your loss is important in changing your perspective from "Isn't this awful" to "This might be good."

No Thinking

DIVORCE CREATES an overload for almost everyone who experiences it. Being a single parent is particularly challenging. I was comforted to read that single parents often forget things and get confused. I thought my having turned 50 was what created my confusion, but no, even young single parents have the problem of circuit overload. How can you get your mind to be calm when you have financial challenges, single parent challenges, loneliness, and extra household duties to overwhelm you? Meditation is the answer for the divorce overload, whether or not you are a parent. With meditation we are not necessarily going for an image. We are trying instead to get our minds to stop all that incessant chatter that goes on in our heads. Here is my quick guide to meditation:

1. Pick a special phrase to repeat. I repeat different things at different times. In a meditation workshop by Judy Stewart, I received a mantra—a phrase or word to repeat when keeping the mind clear. Most of the time I repeat the word given to me at her retreat, but you can use any word you choose. You could use your own name to repeat, as the poet Tennyson did. You may use the word "one," or any word you wish. I like to use a religious phrase or verse from time to time, such as, "Thy will be done," or "Be still and know that I am God." When I am trying to go to sleep, I use one word on the exhalation of my breath (such as "relax") and another word on the inhalation (such as "sleep" or "peace"). For several months I used a phrase to repeat whenever I thought of my ex. I would pray, "God, help me to forgive him." It was very helpful to tie thoughts of my ex to asking for help from a divine source. But the main way I use a mantra is by repeating the phrase to keep my mind clear of thoughts.

2. Find a comfortable place to sit where you will not be disturbed for 30 minutes. Then, do one of three things. You may close your eyes, which is what I do. You may pick a spot on the floor a few feet in front of you to

stare at. Or you might pick something religious to stare at, such as a cross or a picture of a spiritual figure. The point is to find something to do with your eyes. I can keep more thoughts out of my mind with my eyes closed.

3. Begin breathing more deeply than usual. I start by taking three very deep breaths. I hold each breath in for a count of eight before I exhale slowly through my partially closed lips to an eight-count. As I meditate, I track my breath—noticing it going in and noticing it going out. Often I picture my breath going all the way down to my toes as I inhale. Some people like to picture the air going in being one color and the air going out being another. That might be fun for you too, but you might find it generates thoughts.

4. Begin repeating the word over and over for a specified amount of time. I meditate for 30 minutes in the morning and 20 to 30 minutes in mid-afternoon.

5. Casually dismiss thoughts by categorizing them and sending them off. For example, if you notice that you are thinking about the bills, say to yourself, "Thinking about money" and then dismiss the thought. Over the months you will learn what groups of things you are interrupted by, and you will learn more about yourself. You will never get rid of all your thoughts, so don't let that bother you. Just keep sending them gently on their way. You will get better at keeping your mind clear. I have interfering thoughts, however, and I have been doing this

off and on for 20 years! On a good day the thought will be about God and my purpose in His universe; on a bad day the thought will be about whether to select the aqua or iris color for the dress I want to order from the Lands' End catalog.

6. About five minutes before your meditation session ends, picture some goal you have. I want to make a living doing what I love to do most in the world—help people through writing for them, as I am doing now. I know that if my books don't sell, I have not helped anyone and not made a living as a writer, so the image I picture as my goal is a book signing with people lined up to have me sign books. You might choose to imagine health, work success, romance—whatever goal you have. Do that the last few minutes and then gently stop the meditation.

This meditation process heals you from divorce in three ways. First, your mind is stopped from thinking about the divorce for a period of time. The Zen masters talk about the monkey chatter that goes on in our minds all the time—all the useless silly thoughts that crowd our minds and create anxiety. When you can master the monkey chatter, your perspective on life changes. You feel a healthy separation from all those stories, theories about what happened to you and what your ex is like, which we discussed in our first chapter. Remember: Thoughts are just thoughts. You can sit there and watch them come and go, experiencing your mind as something beyond thoughts. It is a very peaceful feeling.

Second, when you apply meditation to all aspects of your daily life, you begin to be aware of your activity in the present rather than being on automatic pilot all day long while your mind stays with the divorce. When you are washing the dishes, you are washing dishes instead of thinking about how glad or mad you are that you got that set of dishes in the divorce. When you are talking to your children, you are actually hearing what they are saying rather than saying, "Yes, honey," while your mind is a thousand miles away. In this way you make your entire day a meditation by not living in monkey chatter, but in what is right there before you.

Third, if your ex is upset about something, you will be able to avoid jumping on the upset wagon with him or her. Lanni is a good example. She had been practicing meditation very diligently for nearly a year when her ex telephoned, screaming and cursing. He was angry that she was taking him back to court to increase the child support. Lanni was extremely impressed with how calm she remained. She had thought some months before, "When he can't upset me, I will be over him," and now it had happened. Lanni felt that it was because of meditation that she was able to be cool in the face of such heat.

Looking at quieting your mind is part of the process of controlling your mind's constant story-creation. First, we considered the idea of mentally and physically standing up to the Divorce Bully that might be pushing you around. Second, we looked at how you might motivate yourself to move on for the sake of others who are affected by your suffering. Third, we examined all the gains created by your loss. Fourth, we attempted to stop those story-making engines of our minds altogether.

If there was ever a time you needed to have your mind be in the best condition it can be, this is it. Think of the mind as the engine that drives your life—controlling your thoughts by opposing your divorce demons; noticing your gains; thinking of others; or silencing your thoughts. Divorce can be the time for a mental tune-up. After you have your story straight enough to put your mind at rest, as chapter one discussed, try to spend as little time as possible thinking about why it all happened. After a certain point, whose fault it was is just not that relevant. Let go of the injustice, because you are not likely to get justice in this situation. It is just like your mother told you about those mosquito bites as a child, "If you pick it, it won't heal." Those bites of disappointment are best left alone. Help your mind stop touching those sore spots.

The New Mind

Choose how you interpret your loss beyond the story. Deliberately think or do not think in helpful ways.

OPPOSITIONAL THINKING:
- Resistance is good, when you resist letting the loss ruin your life

(continued)

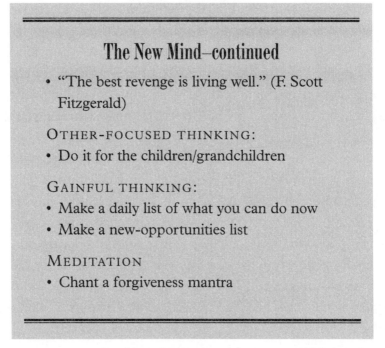

The New Mind—continued

- "The best revenge is living well." (F. Scott Fitzgerald)

OTHER-FOCUSED THINKING:
- Do it for the children/grandchildren

GAINFUL THINKING:
- Make a daily list of what you can do now
- Make a new-opportunities list

MEDITATION
- Chant a forgiveness mantra

CHAPTER SIX

Fake It 'Til You Make It

There is no medicine like hope,
no incentive so great, and no tonic so powerful
as the expectation of something tomorrow.

—O. S. MARDEN

DIVORCE FORCES you into so many new behaviors that it is almost like travel to a foreign land, particularly if you avoid rushing into another relationship. When I divorced the second time, my oldest son made me promise I would date at least 20 men before I remarried. He felt that if I had taken the time to date many men before I married the second time, I would have made a better choice. Whether or not he was right, I agreed that this time I was not going to escape into another marriage. Even though I had a career, I had always felt that my life had been primarily devoted to my man, his career, and our children. I was going to use my new single life as a time to become even more of my own person—to discover who I was, what I wanted, and where I wanted to be. But it took some thinking to know where to begin. Since I had been helping clients explore the same territory from my safe vantage point of the therapy office, it was now my time to see if what I had advocated for my clients worked for me.

Therapists have learned from cognitive–behavioral psychotherapy that when we take an action, the feelings that would normally accompany that action eventually follow. I first noticed this when I was teaching assertiveness classes. When people who did not feel at all assertive would start doing assertive behaviors, they would soon begin to feel that they could and should ask for what they wanted. Since the mid-seventies, I have been encouraging clients in therapy to take the actions consistent with their goals and not worry about how they feel. Invariably, their feelings change when they change their actions.

In Alcoholics Anonymous they have the expression, "Fake it 'til you make it." This captures the essence of what I am suggesting here. Once you have addressed the issues, as you did in chapter one, how do you move on? If you take the actions of a satisfying single life, pretending for a while that your feelings about the divorce are healed, you may find that you are actually pulled forward in your healing process by those actions. One day you may realize that your behavior and feelings match.

WORK ON YOUR SKILL SETS

BEING SINGLE again means you have to do many things for yourself that your mate may have done for you. This is particularly true if you married young, had a long marriage, and raised children. If you had a wife who stayed at home, you may have no idea how to do laundry or make coffee. If you were the stay-at-home wife, you may have no idea where your valuable papers are or what to do when the oil light blinks on in your car. How can you get a grip on all these unfamiliar yet necessary actions?

I have a friend in New York who is a business consultant. We were talking about her job, and she used a piece of jargon that I thought was useful. It was the term "skill sets." I began to think about how that term applied to divorce. What skill sets do you need to develop to create a good single life after divorce? I think they fall into five categories: self-maintenance skills, parenting skills, money-management skills, boundary-setting skills, and social skills.

Self-Maintenance Skills

Research shows that men take divorce harder than women, meaning that they are more likely to commit suicide, check into a mental hospital, or turn to alcohol or drugs. I have always thought that the reason for this was partially that many men do not have the self-maintenance skill set that women have. For example, I recently met a man who had been divorced for 20 years and still didn't know how to cook. "How have you kept from starving?" I asked. "Do you go out to eat every meal?" He replied that he had survived by eating frozen dinners for 20 years. This is scoring low on the self-maintenance test!

If you have grown dependent on someone to take care of you, divorce may be your opportunity to truly become a grown-up for the first time—particularly if you went straight from your parents' house to being married. The self-maintenance skill set includes these basic survival skills:

- maintaining a reasonably healthy eating regimen by preparing most of your foods yourself
- keeping your apartment or house minimally clean and orderly
- keeping your car in good repair
- keeping your wardrobe in decent shape

This may sound simple if you have not been married long, or if you married later in life. But if you have been married since your were 18 years old and always had a marriage with a strong division of labor, learning these simple life skills can be overwhelming at first.

Judy dated Bob and later married him. When they started dating, he was divorced, 30, and living in his mother's basement. When she first saw his basement apartment, she noticed that it was very dusty. She asked how long he had lived there. He reported that he had been there for six months. She said, "When did you last dust?" He said, "I have never dusted." After marrying Bob, she had a great deal of frustration with him because he had not mastered the self-maintenance skills of preparing his own food, maintaining basic order, or cleaning his environment. Essentially, he successfully avoided having to develop this skill set by marrying Judy. This put an enormous burden on her, and as the years went by, she felt she was raising their two children *and* her husband.

Larry was smarter than Bob about self-maintenance. He knew that he was either going to end up living off microwave dinners or learn to cook. He took cooking classes at the local continuing education center. This had two advantages—he mastered the skill of preparing food, and he met women who were interested in preparing food too.

My parents were happily married for 64 years. During the last nine years of my mother's life, she was in a nursing home—now called "an extended-care facility." My mother had been a typical wife of her generation, doing all the housework (although with the help of a housekeeper) and all the cooking. My father impressed me by mastering grocery shopping, cooking, and washing his clothes at age 78. He had a wonderful housekeeper, Barb, who taught him how to run the washing machine and do some basic cooking and light home maintenance.

Little things can take on symbolic proportions when you are first living on your own. Cathy had never pumped her own gas either before or during her marriage, so it was with great trepidation that she stood at the gas pump reading the instructions. She was fearful that she might accidentally spill gas all over the ground, or somehow start a fire that would transform her neighborhood into a conflagration. But she did it. After giving the attendant her $12.75, she felt that her successful gas pumping was a sign that she would able to handle grownup life on her own. Of course, she still needed to find a repair shop for her car that did not leave her feeling robbed after she paid her repair bill. But that is a problem we all face.

New Parenting Skills

You may have some of the skills you need to be a successful parent, but you might find your parenting skill set inadequate in the context of the single-parent role. This is not surprising. In most families one partner is the tough parent and the other is the pushover. When you are taking care of the children all by yourself, even for a weekend, your style may have to change.

I confess: I was the pushover in my first marriage. My job was to make the children feel good and reassure them that they were loved. My first husband's primary parenting job was to maintain law and order. It was a dirty job, but somebody had to do it. When we divorced, I had no choice but to pick up the slack and make sure certain things were done. Where I had been lax before, I became the enforcer of the rules.

As you go through divorce, you will have to move to a more centrist parental style, neither a pushover nor a police sergeant. If you have been the tough task master, you have to back off some, because the kids only have to tolerate that until they are around 12 years old. In most states, at that age they can begin to refuse to visit or live with you. Besides, research has shown repeatedly that neither being very permissive nor being very strict is a good parenting style. Both extremes have been shown to produce juvenile delinquents.

Divorce will create more challenges for you as a single parent than you would have had as an intact family.

The children often have their own upsets to deal with, including additional people to adjust to or rebel against, as in stepparents or step-siblings. Research shows that even 10 years after the divorce, children are likely to harbor resentments. As a single parent you have all the usual things to deal with alone, and then the unusual things to deal with too: resentment toward you or your ex for having "caused" the divorce, the sense of disloyalty the child may feel for liking a stepparent, and your own challenge at not saying negative things about your ex when upsetting situations arise. One of the biggest challenges is knowing your child is exposed to things you consider dangerous or inappropriate.

Kate came from an alcoholic family but was not a drinker herself. Her ex-husband's drinking had been one of the reasons she left the marriage, and now she had to send her son, Peter, every other weekend to a home where she knew there would be heavy drinking. Kate had to walk that fine line between making Peter suspicious of every beer his father had, and informing the seven-year-old when to call her rather than get in the car with his father. Kate handled this by always offering to pick up and deliver Peter, but she could not control what happened in between pickup and delivery. As Peter got older, she could talk to him about drinking and ask him to call when he needed a ride. As a therapist, I have been involved in helping divorced husbands and wives deal with a drinking spouse in this situation. Unless the ex has a record of arrests for driving while intoxicated, there is not much that the nondrinking parent can do, other than educate the child. This is difficult without negatively labeling the child's other parent.

Sometimes you may disapprove of the way the other parent handles the child's feeding and bathing. Danny had custody of his five-year-old son, Travis. He felt upset when, week after week, he would pick the boy up from his ex-wife's and find him wearing the same outfit he had worn three days earlier when Danny had dropped the boy off. In this situation, you may request that your ex change his or her behavior, but often you have no choice but to deal with the child and hope he or she will learn more self-maintenance skills. These situations are part of the additional upsets that you may have as a parent.

I was lucky with my first husband because our values and habits were very similar and we banded together as parents for the sake of the children. If a child was grounded at my house, the grounding would continue at the other parent's house. Unfortunately, such cooperation is not the rule, but it is a goal to achieve if you and your ex can manage. If you have children, negotiating with someone you might not feel that positive about is another skill that divorce requires.

Parenting alone is not easy; but I feel that the experience of being a parent is the most personally rewarding experience of my life, and I know I am not alone in this. Recently, I was faced with the choice of going on a trip with a man or keeping my plans to visit my daughter in Oakland. I chose my daughter without a second thought. When a friend asked why I didn't cancel my California trip, I replied, "So far, men have been temporary experiences. Children are forever." Children are the consistent thread in life for most people. Even if you are not the custodial parent, children often provide the most consistent opportunity to make a difference in the world that will endure after we are gone. Devoting yourself to excellence in parenting skills is probably the most important contribution we ever make to the world.

Financial Mastery Skills

Your relationship to money suddenly changes when you divorce. If you were the impulsive one, you are welcome to plunge yourself into debt with no one to blame but yourself. If you were the frugal one, you now have that chance to save, save, save that you have always wanted. I remember feeling a great deal of freedom, particularly after my first divorce, when I could just go to the ice cream shop without having to feel accountable to anyone else. In that marriage, I had been the spender. In my second marriage, however, the roles were reversed. Whatever your style, you will likely need to adjust your money-management skills after divorce.

Donna had a degree in nursing, but had primarily devoted herself to her children for the last 15 years. When her husband divorced her, she updated her license and began working much harder on her career. She lived frugally, but not without the fun of trips and a nice home, carefully putting money away for retirement. After her future had some security and her children were through college, she opened her own business and devoted herself even more diligently to her career. She seems to be enjoying life. I often think of Donna as a role model. Live with some reserve on the spending, invest wisely, and work hard.

You are now in charge of your money, so money management is a skill set you must master. After my second divorce, I took great joy and satisfaction in learning how to get on the Internet and buy stocks for the first time. A novice to financial matters, I found guidance reading Jane Bryant Quinn's *Making the Most of Your Money*. Perhaps you can take classes on investments, start to live on a budget, or begin to regularly save, even $50 a month. This is the time to make changes now that you have the control over your destiny.

Boundary-Setting Skills

Setting firm boundaries in your relationship with your parents and siblings is another skill set you will probably need to master after divorce. Since we state in the marriage ceremony that the parent gives their daughter to her husband—which I feel is an ancient and outmoded practice, since daughters are not property to be traded—the wedding ceremony itself is a seed for future confusion, especially for women. Men, however, are not exempt, and often want to let their mothers take over the role they alotted to their wives.

Parents are often very confused by their children's divorces. They feel some responsibility and guilt over the divorce, and can't decide whether to be tough with their children or take them back home like prodigal children. Most commonly, parents increase their involvement in the adult child's life, particularly if there are grandchildren. This is certainly not bad, but as the divorcing person, you find yourself going through what you did when you were an adolescent and moved out for the first time: establishing boundaries between yourself and your parents.

Jim and his mother usually talked once a week on Sundays and, although Jim had not spilled his guts to his mother, she had known Jim and Alexis were breaking up for a long time. Alexis had dropped hints, and finally Jim had told his mother they were going to separate. "Honey, do you want to come and live with me for a while?" Jim knew this was a likely invitation and he had considered the possibility.

"Mom, I just don't think that would be a great idea. I remember when I moved back home after college when I was looking for a job. I think I regressed and it made it harder for me to stand on my own two feet. When you started to take care of me again, I stopped being a man. I really appreciate your caring, but I have made plans to move into Fred's apartment complex near the office."

His mother was understanding about his position. In the long run Jim did spend some more time with his mother, but he maintained his independence and did not find himself regressing to boyhood patterns.

Krissy's parents had money—plenty of money. When she let them know that she and Mike were ending their 10-year marriage, they began almost to seduce her into returning to the nest. "Why don't you move here? We could give you our rental property to live in—the tenant's lease is almost up. You could sell your van and use our Buick. We don't really need a third car." Krissy could feel herself being sucked into a dependent position, losing control of her life. It took all the courage she had to resist their offers, but she knew that those offers came with conditions. She had married Mike to get away from her parents' control, and she knew better than to give in. She knew what would come next: their opinions about how she should raise the kids, whom she should date, and which church she should attend. Krissy resisted.

I am not saying parents should never help. Rae was nearly killed by her abusive husband. He was getting ready to go out for the evening and was standing at the mirror shaving when she said, "Give me a minute and I'll go with you." Suddenly enraged, he slashed her throat with the straight razor he was shaving with. She grabbed a towel, pressed it to the wound, and drove herself to the hospital, passing out in the parking lot. Fortunately, someone found her and saved her life. After three days in the hospital, she called her parents. Her father said, "You made your bed, now lie in it. We will not come and get you." She escaped and started her life over all by herself. Twenty years later, she is one of the happiest and most successful women I know, but that was a time when parents should have stuck their noses in their child's business.

Set boundaries, but don't turn down appropriate support or free babysitting. I have a lot of pride. My parents offered to help me out financially after my first divorce, but I insisted on gutting it out on my own. After my second divorce, I allowed them to help me with the Texas move. They were always respectful of boundaries, and I am very grateful for the no-strings-attached help I received. If your parents offer help, just ask yourself two questions: Will there be a price to pay now or later? Will this keep me from discovering my strength? If the answer to both of these is no, then accept the help.

Social Mastery Skills

Divorce tosses your friendships up in the air like a bunch of feathers. Whether they land near you or are blown away takes months to sort out. As people often comment, you find out who your real friends are in a divorce. But even if you have friends who stick by you, most of those friends are married and it feels uncomfortable to always be the single friend in a group of married people.

One of the most important skill sets to create when you are starting a single life is to master making friends. Fortunately for you, if not for families and children involved, divorce is now so common that you are not alone. But how can you meet people?

I've already discussed the benefits of singles' groups, but if you do not want to go to join one, no problem. Make a list of all the things you like to do and rate them as to the likelihood that you will meet other people with those interests. For example, if your interest is cooking, you are not likely to meet people unless you take a class. If you like to read, most bookstores have classes and book events going on all the time. If you like sports, most communities have sports clubs whose primary members are singles. You must get out of your house to meet people, and that takes courage the first few times.

Recently I attended a singles' adult class where I was a newcomer. When someone said to me, "It's hard to come the first time," I realized that it didn't bother me at all. I was really struck by how differently I would have felt three years ago. I moved to a new city a year and a half after my husband had left, and I knew only a couple of married friends. The thought of going somewhere alone, particularly into a singles' group, was very hard at first. Now I feel no anxiety other than wondering if I will be able to find the location, because it is so hard to find your way around Dallas.

How did I overcome those fears? Over and over again, I made myself go out. I went to singles' groups, concerts, church groups, sailing clubs, classes, restaurants, and bookstore events. I didn't wait until I had a friend to go with me. I often went by myself and had wonderful adventures. For example, I went to a Rachmaninoff piano concert, where the sponsor announced that everyone was welcome to join the pianist afterward for a dinner. I thought, "Sure. That would be a great chance to meet people." When I went to dinner, I was fortunate to sit next to the very talented pianist, and we became friends and later corresponded. If I had stayed home because I had no one to go with, that would never have happened. Now I have a network of single friends, and I know I never have to spend a weekend alone, unless I want to.

Single life may be a little harder again for men because they are usually expected to initiate dating. My second husband confessed to me after we were engaged that he had never called up anyone in his life and asked her on a date. Even though he had been married before, all his relationships had been like ours, where he and a woman started hanging out together and just sort of fell into a romantic involvement. He had not mastered the dating skill set. Men, I suggest you view asking women out in the same way you might view applying for a job. You know that you will not get every job you apply for, you expect some rejection, and you may even apply for jobs you really don't want that much just to have practice at the interview process. The more you practice at anything, the easier it gets.

This advice applies to women as well. I have frequently found excellent excuses to ask men out. It could be business-related events, or the invitation could be stated as a would-you-mind-being-my-escort invitation. I asked out my first husband. I knew he liked basketball, and I was between boyfriends. I called him up to ask him if we could go to the college basketball game together, and he invited me to dinner before the game. We were at the University of Kansas and it was a Nebraska–Kansas game, a hot rivalry. Ten months later we were married, but we had known each other as casual friends for over a year and a half. Contrary to what you may have heard, it does not ruin everything to pursue a man. If someone interests me, I do not hesitate to pursue. Go for it!

I meet people everywhere—in the grocery store, at church, in line at the airport, everywhere—because I smile and make eye contact. I am interested and curious about people. (A good book on this topic is *Be Your Own Dating Service*, by Nina Atwood.)

You can begin a conversation in at least three ways. You can make a comment about the other person. Last weekend, as I was purchasing a computer program, the man in line behind me made a comment on the program and we began talking. You can ask for information, such as asking for directions or a recommendation for a nearby restaurant for lunch. You can make a comment about the environment, such as the weather. There are plenty of ways to develop those flirting skills. If you really need some remedial training, there are always Dale Carnegie courses.

The social skill set you are developing is called "initiating relationships with both sexes" and "creating a social network." These are essential skills. If you are still wondering what to do, find someone you know who is good at these things and observe what he or she does.

Lisa had been married for 15 years. Now her divorce was final and she did not have the slightest idea how to start dating again. Luckily for Lisa, her friend from high school, Nancy, had always been a consummate flirt and had never married. Lisa asked if she and Nancy could go out together. Nancy gave Lisa the advance course in flirting. Although Lisa was still shy, she now had some ideas about eye contact and conversation starters she could use in various settings.

Set yourself a goal to make conversation with at least one stranger a week. You are not trying to find the love of your life. You are only practicing making conversation. This is the attitude I use at singles' dances. I am not going to fall in love. I am only going out to be with people and hear the music. I usually have a great time and I have often met someone I ended up dating.

With all the possibilities in the world, you can find someone to be your partner. If you have ever thought you have to be thin, rich, handsome, or beautiful to have a partner, just go to the mall and watch couples. They are not all paired with flawless people. Besides, those men and women out there are a lot like you. They want fun and comfort just the way you do. They have often been hurt just as you have. They need approval in the same way you need approval.

ACTION PRINCIPLES

IN THE first part of this chapter, we looked at the skill sets that are necessary for creating a satisfying single life. But there is a more abstract way to assess what actions to take after divorce. Three questions can guide you to healing actions: What if the divorce were no longer a problem? What do others do? What did you do before?

What If the Divorce
Were No Longer a Problem?

My specialty is short-term therapy—helping people recover quickly from the difficulty that brought them into
therapy. One of the questions I ask my clients is, "What
will you be doing when this is no longer a problem?"
This question can suggest actions that will help you heal
from your divorce. Once you decide what you would be
doing, you can go ahead and take those actions that will
lead to your future.

I woke up on a Saturday morning dreading facing another weekend day without my husband, who had been
gone for a month. I wanted to pull the covers over my head
and not emerge until Monday morning. I asked myself,
What would I do today if I didn't feel this way? Normally, I
got up and fixed waffles for the children on Saturdays.
Then I would do a couple of loads of laundry, shop a little,
and maybe rent a movie for the evening. Even though I did
not feel at all like doing those things, I did drag myself out
of bed and head toward the waffle iron. As I started doing
the non-misery things, I began to feel less miserable.

What Do Others Do?

I have met men and women who seemed quite delighted
to be single. They love the freedom to come and go as
they please and don't see their lives as lacking because
they do not have a mate. This is particularly true of

people who have children, and therefore have their connection needs met by the family. I have asked them about their lives and copied some of their behaviors.

Janet is a particularly good example. She divorced in her forties. She took the freedom from marriage as an opportunity to do two things: work on her career and travel. She had always wanted to go to Europe to see some of the art there, particularly in Italy. She planned a three-week-long tour and used some of her settlement money for the occasion.

James thought, "If I were over my divorce I would have a network of friends to hang out with." However, he could not find a place to do that other than a bar, which was not interesting to him. He decided that his community needed a singles' organization. He filled up his life with creating a network of people through churches to create a Christian singles' organization in his community. His answer to the question "What would you do if you were over your divorce?" helped many people.

Maybe what you would do if you were over your divorce is something as simple as attend church, call friends, or eat more healthily. But whatever you consider healed actions, those are the actions you should begin to take right now.

What Did You Do Before?

Earlier, we talked about using images of what you did before marriage to enhance your future imagination. Here, we are considering your actions previous to marriage.

What activities did you participate in before you were married to lead an enjoyable, fulfilling life? Most of us can remember the life we had before marriage and recall some fun, adventuresome, or productive things we used to do before we were someone's spouse. Often these are things we have given up because our spouse was not all that interested in doing what we enjoyed.

Matt used to enjoy golf as a teenager and as a young adult. But when he and Jenny married, Jenny resented his being gone for the number of hours that golf could consume. So Matt stopped playing golf. One of the first things Matt did when he moved out was clean up his clubs and head to the course to play a few holes.

Barb had stopped going to church when she got involved with Sam. He had been raised Catholic and was still resentful over the physical abuse he had received at the hands of the nuns. As a consequence, both Barb and Sam simply did not attend church. After her divorce, one of the what-you-used-to-do-as-a-single-person actions for Barb was to start exploring churches to find a place she would enjoy.

Do It Anyway

I KNOW you may not feel like doing anything, if you are recently divorced. It may be that you're afraid or overwhelmed, or just plain too depressed to do anything right now. You have to make a commitment to yourself to act, no matter how much you feel like hiding out. It is a matter of who will be in charge: the wiser part of you, or your emotions. It may be helpful to separate feelings from doing in your mind. For example, if you think you are too shy to go to a singles' group, tell yourself that you can feel shy and still not act shy. You can feel depressed and still not act depressed.

Sam had not been on a date in 14 years. Now he was faced with dating. Although Sam ran his own company and was confident in his business, talking to women he might date was an overwhelming prospect. In spite of his fears, he made himself go to a local singles' group, Singles-In-Action. Walking up to the door of someone's home to attend "game night" was tough, but he did it anyway. Before the night was over, he had met two women he ended up seeing again. He had felt fear and stepped over it to success.

The good news is that taking the actions of recovery will lead to the feelings of recovery. The sooner you take action, the sooner you will feel better.

Action Hints

Divorce is much more than getting rid of something. It is building something new and requires a set of skills to create a good single life for yourself.

SKILL SETS:
- Self-Maintenance Skills: You may learn to cook, clean, or take care of your car
- Parenting Skills: Raising children is often done in a balance with another party. When you are parenting alone, you may need to change your parenting style
- Money-Management Skills: Divorce is usually a financial disaster. You may need to go back to the basics in managing your money
- Boundary-Setting Skills: Since divorce throws you into a confusing relationship with your parents and perhaps your children, you will need to set boundaries with them
- Social Skills: When you have not dated for years, dating again and making new friends is a great challenge

GENERAL GUIDELINES:
- Ask yourself: What would you be doing if the divorce were no longer a problem?
- Ask yourself: What do successful divorced people do?
- Ask yourself: What did you do before you were married?
- Even if you are afraid, do it anyway

CHAPTER SEVEN

Love,
the Best Cure of All

The other side of anger,
if we experience its emptiness and go through it,
is always compassion.
—CHARLOTTE JOKO BECK

I HAVE TRIED not to emphasize my own experiences in divorce as the how-to or how-not-to of divorce recovery, but there is no way I can discuss spirituality without talking about my own journey. I can only share with you the distance I have gone, as long or short as that has been.

More than anything else, my second divorce threw me into a crisis about why I was here on this planet. I had been raised in a Christian home that emphasized service to others. I had felt God clearly had the mission for me to help couples. I had written two books on marriage with my second husband, taught thousands of couples in a relationship class, and was primarily known for my work with couples. Divorce was not only a deep personal loss, it crushed my dream of having our marriage be a beacon for other couples. Like many who go through divorce, I questioned not only my beliefs about my husband, my judgment in marrying him, and the nature of marriage, but my beliefs about God. Through my struggle with these issues, I reestablished my values about what is important in life and how to manage disappointment and suffering.

What do other traditions have to teach us about suffering? I spent much of the last three years reading about mysticism, Christian or otherwise, and Zen Buddhism. I read about mysticism because I wanted to have more of an experience of the divine rather than an intellectual understanding. I read about Zen because I found many comforts in it and some strategies for managing the present. Some principles from Zen seemed especially important in recovering from divorce: suffering, detachment, living in the present, and compassion.

SUFFERING

BUDDHA SAID that life is suffering, that life is ten thousand sorrows and ten thousand joys. Loosely translated, when you sign up to be reincarnated as a human, you sign up for some suffering. I found great comfort in this. Many of us are raised in sheltered environments and do not anticipate that suffering. We think, as I had, that if we are good people and try not to inflict any pain on others, life will go well. But in reality, suffering, pain, and disappointments will come your way no matter how honorable and good you try to be. I found this concept very comforting when I was faced with the end of my second marriage. This is just life, and suffering was bound to happen one way or another.

In Buddhism there is a story of a woman who came to Buddha holding her dead baby in her arms. She said, "Master, I have heard you can bring people back to life. Please, will you bring my baby back to life?" Buddha told her he would as soon as she brought him a mustard seed from a household where there had been no suffering from death. She went from house to house trying to find a home where there had been no such terrible loss. When she could not, she understood Buddha's point that life includes suffering, and she returned to him ready to bury her baby. She became the Buddha's student.

When we are faced with shocking disappointment, we tend to notice that events occurring in people's lives seem to be determined by fate. Fate can be something unpleasant, such as a car accident; but it can also be something pleasant. If Jan hadn't run out of gas near the hospital, she would not have met her future husband, Dr. Bob. Fortunately, Bob was leaving the hospital after a late round of visits when he noticed her standing by her car with the hood up. She was upset with herself for being so oblivious, but Bob was reassuring and offered to let her use his cellular phone to call someone. When she told him what the problem was, he offered to go get her some gas. He returned 10 minutes later in his white Mercedes, which seemed to Jan to be a white charger. He was rescuing the damsel in distress. That began a great relationship for both of them.

In *Man's Search for Meaning*, Victor Frankl, a Nazi concentration camp prisoner for years, said that he noticed how little quirks of fate determine whether people live or die. He wrote that life is like the Persian story about a man whose servant came to him terrified. The servant said that Death had come to call on him and was coming for him tomorrow. The servant pleaded with his master for his fastest horse so he could ride to Teheran to escape Death. The master gave the servant his fastest horse, and off he went. The next day Death visited the master and the master asked, "Why did you scare my servant so?" Death answered, "I was so surprised to see him here. I am to meet him tonight in Teheran."

Who is to say why you or I went through a divorce? Why did you pick the mate you did? Maybe it was because that person had a lesson for you to learn in life. Maybe it was to slow down your life so that you would be available to be with the person with whom you will spend your last days. Perhaps you chose that person to work through some issue from your childhood. Maybe it was your karma. Or maybe the explanation is as simple as divorce has become an unfortunate way of life for Western culture. Who can really say?

For whatever reason, suffering through divorce or otherwise does seem to be part of life. As I have gotten older, I have seen many of the people I used to envy (because they had not had a divorce) suffer in ways that I have not. They had problems with children, parents, careers, or their health. It does seem that life has suffering and, thank goodness, joys as well.

DETACHMENT

ONE OF the most important lessons of my second divorce was to not be attached to how others saw me. When our divorce appeared in the paper in Omaha, where we lived, I received a call from a local newspaper reporter. He had interviewed my ex and interviewed me. Since just months before we had been on the *Today Show* together for our book on marriage, our divorce was hot news. When the reporter released his story in the local paper, it went out on the Associated Press wire and inevitably appeared in newspapers all over the country. I had previously been sensitive to what others thought of me. This definitely got me over that! Of course, I did feel humbled by the whole experience. Just when you think you have the answers, you might discover you are wrong.

Zen points out that our suffering is mostly caused by our attachment to our ideas. When you are attached to how you think life should be, how you think you ought to be, or how others should behave, you are setting yourself up for pain. Detachment means that you let go of your preconceived notions and expectations. If you think your ex should act in a certain way toward your kids, if you think your kids should be outraged at what their other parent has done, if you think your friends should act in certain ways toward your ex, you are in a position for disappointment.

Charlotte Joko Beck, in her book *Everyday Zen*, uses the analogy of rowing a boat in the fog. Suddenly, another boat comes out of the fog and hits your boat. Just as you start to rage against your fellow boater, you realize that there is no one in the boat. So you simply take care of repairing the hole without all the drama of trying to straighten up the other sailor. This is how you could choose to react to others' flaws when you are going through divorce. Why be attached to how others should be behaving? You only have control over how you behave and you are completely responsible for that.

I had occasion to practice this myself. I received a fax asking if my youngest son could spend Mother's Day with his father, due to a break in his work schedule. I faxed back saying I was fine with that, particularly since I needed to have the boy for Father's Day. We were supposed to have the child on the appropriate parent's day, according to the decree. I was invited to teach in Europe, and thought it would be a great opportunity for my 10-year-old to go with me, but it fell in late June. My former husband called me, cursing and raising his voice on the phone about the plans for Europe. I was pleasantly surprised to find myself not getting upset about what he was saying. I think there were two reasons I was so calm. First, I had been practicing meditation. Second, I had been working on this concept of detachment. I no longer took things personally, even when someone was trying to make the issue personal. I apologized and offered compromises, but we still ended up in court over the trip.

You will know that you have gotten much farther along in your divorce when what your ex does annoys you less. I am certain that you have seen many divorced couples where one partner would continue to keep the court battle going or continue to go out of their way to annoy the other partner, seemingly just to keep the dialog going one way or another. The best way to handle this is to react as little as possible and only do what you have to do legally. Court battles may be a sign that one partner is not emotionally letting go of the situation. These battles can be very upsetting for the children.

In the first chapter, you learned to construct a story about why the divorce happened. I have noticed that the stories that evolve later seem to move toward a less attached version of "why." Pam and Greg were both attorneys, and Pam originally thought that Greg had left her because he was addicted to sex. In fact, he described himself as sexually addicted and he left her because he knew that he could not stop having affairs. She thought this was because he had been sexually abused as a child. There was some truth to that, but after two years I noticed that Pam developed another story. When Greg later married a waitress, Pam came to believe that Greg had been jealous of her success as an attorney. Now he had a wife who could never compete with him professionally.

When another couple of years passed, Pam's story softened even more as she thought that if she had been raised in the same family and abused when she was a child, perhaps she would have been just as incapable of fidelity as her husband. I liked the more compassionate version she espoused about Greg's fidelity. She concluded that Greg was doing the best he could, and, unfortunately for their children, this was it.

Although you cannot rush your feelings too much, I have seen many clients detach from rejection by looking at the overall context of the exiting spouse's life. Mary and Tom had been married for 25 years. When their daughter married, Tom moved in with a woman 15 years younger than he. Mary concluded that the prospect of becoming a grandfather was more than Tom could face, detaching Mary's understanding from anything personal about Mary. People do often leave a marriage for age issues that have nothing to do with the attractiveness of the spouse.

Detachment is similar to the idea of turning something over to God. A psychologist friend and I were discussing my frustration that, although I had dated many men, I had found no one special. She suggested that I turn this over to God. Her method when she was divorced was to buy a pretty jar, which she called her "God jar," and to put a list of what she wanted in the jar. This stressed stepmother joked that she forgot to include "no children" on that list. I thought I would try this too. I made a list of over a dozen characteristics of my future mate, which included things like: enjoys reading, loves food, spiritual, honest, and so on. I decided to put them all on slips of paper, since I could not select which was most important. With a prayer, I dropped them into the jar. One of the tiny slips of paper missed the jar. Oops! That's not good, I thought as I looked at the tiny slip of paper that was face down on the carpet. I picked it up and turned it over. It had written on it, "Likes sex and can still perform." I hope I won't later think of this as an omen. No matter whether you use a God jar or detachment, you will have significant peace if you can let go of how things should be now and in the future.

LIVING IN THE PRESENT: THE GIFT

HAS IT ever struck you that "present," in terms of time, is the same word we use for a "gift" we give to someone? When you go through a divorce, it is so easy to be anywhere but the present. You can be roaming around the past for explanations and justifications for the divorce. But you can also be dreaming that things will be wonderful in the future, either when you get to be with someone you know now or find someone whom you are imagining will be terrific.

I know that hope is one of the things that lifts us from the pain of divorce or of any situation. But have you ever considered that hope is perhaps not as great as it is reputed to be? Could it be that hope is a negation of the present that God has given us?

One of the concepts I like in Zen philosophy is the emphasis on making your whole life a meditation by being aware of what you are doing in the present. Whatever you are doing, avoid thinking, "I'll just get this over with so I can do the next thing I want to do." Consider a task like mowing the lawn. Rather than noticing the smell of the freshly cut grass, the warmth of the sunlight on your body, or the satisfaction of creating order, you may be thinking, "I'll just get this over with so I can go shopping or have a beer or catch the game on television." You are not really mowing the lawn. You are somewhere else. On a larger scale, rather than noticing what is great about this day, you may be thinking how horrible it is to face everything alone now that you are not married, or that life will be fine when you get involved with your next mate. That is the opposite of being in the here and now.

You may be thinking, "Good idea. But how do I do it?" I have made a considerable effort to stay in the present in the last couple of years, and I have found the main tool for being present-oriented is to focus on your senses. What are you seeing, hearing, feeling, or smelling now? Now? Now? Of course, we do spend most of our lives not being conscious of our present experience, but thinking, thinking, thinking. Noticing what your senses experience every minute is a way to heal from your divorce. You can fill up your mind with something better than trying to figure out why or yearning for something different to be happening.

This is an extension of your meditation, because when you meditate you are aware of the present in much the same way. For example, you may be following your breath in and out and noticing the way thoughts try to fill up your mind as you are trying to empty it. You take charge of your experience in meditation and remain in the present, which is exactly how you will heal from your divorce. When you take charge of your thinking, you take charge of your life even without making major changes in your external circumstances.

Perhaps because so many things besides divorce piled up on me at once—the closing of my business, a lawsuit against one of the therapists I supervised, a son leaving for college, my mother's death, and the placement of my father in an assisted-living facility—I needed some real answers as to why we are here on this planet and why we suffer. All these events happened within two years from the date of the divorce. Loss and tragedy are what lead us to a deeper spirituality. Although I had an excellent therapist and many loving friends, my sense of a relationship with God was what steadied me through the losses. I reconnected with church, although most of my guidance came through my reading and prayer. I felt a yearning not to be back in a relationship with a person, but to feel connected with a higher loving force—God. That helped me focus on compassion.

COMPASSION

WHAT I like about both Christianity and Buddhism is the emphasis on compassion for your fellow human beings. Being able to put yourself in someone else's place, even your ex's, and have compassion for that person is one of the ways I hope your divorce will ultimately contribute to your growth. Feeling compassion is like an emotional barometer as to how far along you are on your recovery.

Both Buddhism and Christianity stress compassion for yourself. We often blame ourselves for the divorce and then pick on ourselves for not being able to get over it more quickly. You can't love your neighbor as yourself if you do not love yourself. You may fear falling into a pit of self-pity, but instead you can give yourself some credit and compassion. Here's the credit: You bought this book. You are taking healing steps. Now, what can you do to show yourself some compassion? Would it be accepting yourself as a human, with all the emotional scars and wrinkles that implies? Would it be saying to yourself, as you would to a friend, "You did the best you could at the time"? Give yourself some compassion, and let it flow to others.

When you first divorce, it is nearly impossible to look past your own pain and see anyone else's. It seemed to me that the first compassion I felt was for my children. Children of divorce have their lives turned upside down. Often they have to leave the house they considered home. Their daily lives are disrupted by thoughts of which parent they are supposed to be with now. All holidays are marred by trying to keep both parents happy for the rest of their lives. Divorce may be a wonderful opportunity for a parent to have a new relationship or a new life without the burdens of a relationship, but it is not a fresh, exciting start for a child. The more compassion you can have for your children, and the fewer demands you can put on them to fill your life, the better.

Next my compassion extended to my parents. I could put myself in their shoes. I knew they must feel embarrassed over my divorce, particularly as it was the second time. No one in my family had ever divorced. (Of course, there were very few people to mar this tradition, since I am the only married offspring from seven married adults in the last generation!) I tried to imagine how difficult it must have been to say to their friends who asked about me, "She's divorced again." They alleged that this was not a problem for them, but I wondered.

Eventually, I was able to extend my awareness outside my family and feel compassion for my former spouse. Compassion for your spouse may not be something you can tackle before you go to court, but the sooner you get to it after court, the better. The more you can extend compassion to all your fellow human beings, the sooner you will be healed from your divorce.

John came to therapy because he was still suffering from his divorce, although it had been almost two years. His ex had moved away and taken their child with her. He searched on the Internet for the opportunity to volunteer to help others as part of his recovery. He selected the chance to work with handicapped children as part of his recovery. He said helping kids whose bodies created such barriers for them put everything in perspective for him. He discovered his ability to be compassionate and found a way to put his suffering behind him by serving others.

I recently attended a lecture by Dannion Brinkley, who had two near-death experiences. He had been dead for over 20 minutes and was on the way to the morgue when he came back the first time. He learned that love is what our whole existence is about, a concept echoed in most of the major religions. His suggestion was that each of us become healers, if even in a small way.

As you finish this book, I hope you'll look for a way to become a healer. Whether you volunteer to work with the dying, the sick, or with children, the goal is to make your life a contribution to others. Maybe you want to start small, such as volunteering to feed your neighbors' cat when they are out of town, shoveling snow for an older relative, or even something as small and planet-loving as picking up the trash someone threw out of their car—even if it didn't fall in your yard. I once heard that the genius architect Buckminster Fuller would pick up toilet paper off the floor of public bathrooms as part of his commitment to the planet. When I am walking in my neighborhood, as I do most mornings, and I see several papers on an absent neighbor's driveway, I gather them up and hide them on the neighbor's stoop. Little things are a good start.

When you can reach outside yourself and devote yourself to healing, you may discover how much you have to give to others and you will heal more quickly from divorce because your own suffering will be put in perspective by your service.

So often we think of love in romantic terms. Though there is some level of healing that cannot occur without being in a relationship, it saddens me to see people attempt to escape their pain by leaping into another relationship.

Wiley had been divorced less than three months when he met Cindy. He fell instantly in love with her, but I was skeptical about how much of his feelings were a rush of dependency instead of a rush of true love. He needed to know where she was every minute, and began pushing for a commitment. Wiley's neediness was born from the deep rejection he felt in the divorce. Because he wanted to escape those feelings, he would constantly ask Cindy for reassurance that he was lovable. This kind of love is not going to heal you from divorce. It is a demanding love that sucks the life out of a relationship. This is not the level of love I am talking about.

When I divorced the second time, one of the thoughts I had was that I did have a lot of love to give. Now I had fewer opportunities, other than my children and my parents. I had devoted much of my time to the marriage. I came to see the divorce as an opportunity to express my love in a larger way. My new mission is to devote myself to helping divorcing people heal and to loving in a more universal way.

Often, as I drive down the highway under the vast stretches of blue Texas sky, I am in awe of how lucky I am. I live where I have always wanted to live. I do what I love for a living—therapy, teaching, writing. I have wonderful children, of whom I am very proud. I had a great childhood with loving parents who were very positive models for me. Even though twice I have faced the disappointments and suffering from divorce, my life has been blessed with much joy and a sense of purpose. That purpose has been to help you find some answers. Take the ones that work for you and let the others drift away.

At the beginning of this book, I quoted a line from the movie *Shadowlands*, in which C. S. Lewis asked a student, "Do you think we read so that we will not feel alone?" I hope that you have found many practical answers to the ways to get over a divorce more quickly and you have realized that you are not alone. Others have suffered on this same journey and recovered. I hope the shared wisdom of my clients and the many teachers I have had in books and in life will make your journey to recovery from divorce a shorter one than it otherwise would have been. Best wishes to you, Healer.

Compassion

Make peace by focusing on detachment, and living in the present, and loving others.

DETACHMENT:
- Do not take things personally
- Let go of how things "should" be

LIVING IN THE PRESENT:
- Be aware of your senses
- Be in every experience

LOVING OTHERS:
- Work with those in need
- Have compassion

APPENDIX A:
Choosing a
Good Therapist

Because so many people, when going through a divorce, ask me how to pick a therapist, I thought it fitting to make a few suggestions.

First, let's talk about the various types of therapists that are available. There are psychiatrists, psychologists, social workers, certified counselors, and pastoral counselors. All of these titles require special training and each contains both competent and incompetent members of the profession. Nowadays, for most people, whom you see most likely depends on who your insurance covers. One of the good things about this is that the list of providers you are allowed to see has been screened by your managed care company. A good recommendation is very helpful when you are selecting a therapist. Besides using your provider list as a resource, you can ask friends who have gone to therapy; pastors, priests, and rabbis; or even your primary care physician may have a recommendation. Many clients who have come to my counseling center referred themselves after looking in the telephone book; however, I recommend getting a more personal referral before finding a doctor or therapist through an ad.

There are national accrediting organizations for various specialty groups in therapy. In the past, I have been most satisfied with therapists approved by the American Association for Marriage and Family Therapy when it comes to working with divorce issues, because I know they have all been trained in family issues, particularly single-parent issues. You may call the American Association for Marriage and Family Therapy at their national referral number to get a suggestion for a therapist: (202) 452-0109.

There is a confidentiality rule that applies to all therapists and their clients. This rule means everything you tell your therapist is kept completely confidential at all times. However, you should be aware that there are three different cases where the therapist may legally break confidentiality (tell someone something you have told them in confidence). One of these cases is when your medical records are subpoenaed for court. Another is if the therapist believes you may harm yourself or someone else— such as in a case of suicide or homicide. Lastly, your therapist may legally break the confidentiality rule if there is reason to believe that a child in therapy or a child in association with the client is being physically or sexually abused.

What personal characteristics should you look for in a therapist? I joke that I have finally become the therapist I would want to go to—someone with life experience who has suffered a little herself and made it to the other side. But personally, I would prefer someone a little older who has been married for some time, and maybe divorced, but not too many times. (I joke that I have had 26 years of cumulative marital experience.) The most important thing is that you feel comfortable with your therapist. If you can communicate comfortably and feel that what you're receiving is helpful to you, that should be enough. When it comes to therapeutic approaches, I am leery of therapists who say they are searching for underlying causes. What made us the way we are is usually not so obscure or challenging as training ourselves to stop following unproductive patterns. I would prefer a therapist who says they are solution-oriented, solution focused, goal-oriented, or cognitive behavioral. Therapists working with these approaches tend to focus on the goals the clients set as well as on the strengths and resources of the clients, and often the duration of the treatment is less. By seeking a therapist with these models as his or her basis for working with you, you are more likely to avoid unnecessary sessions. If you begin therapy and the therapist seems to bring up more and more things that he or she thinks you should work on, look out. Go into therapy with your own agenda and pursue what *you* want to change.

If you are interested in having a telephone session with me, my toll-free number for arranging this is (800) 234-4076. Although I prefer face-to-face therapy, telephone work is always an option if you have trouble finding someone in your area.

APPENDIX B:
Recommended Reading

There are about 250 titles in print about divorce and the loss of a love. Since you may want to read a few other books on these subjects, here is a short, manageable list with some descriptions that might be helpful.

Judith Viorst's *Necessary Losses* (Ballantine Books) points out that growth and change are inevitable and deals with the expectations we have going into relationships. There are four sections in this book, and the last one expands upon letting go.

Abigail Trafford's *Crazy Time* (Harperperennial Library) deals with the stages of processes and includes actual exercises. It is a what-to-expect book with an emphasis on normalizing the reader's feelings.

Catherine Napolitane and Victoria Pellegrino's *Living and Loving After Divorce* (New American Library) walks the line between describing stages, telling you what to expect and what to avoid, and giving practical advice.

A classic in the field of divorce is Constance Ahrons's *The Good Divorce* (Basic Books). This book is based on the research the author has conducted at the University of Southern California about divorcing families that succeed in meeting children's needs.

Two books by Melinda Blau that I particularly enjoyed serve as daily inspirations for parents rebuilding their lives after divorce. One is called *Loving and Listening* (Perigee) and the other is her guide for parents who are divorcing entitled *Families Apart: Ten Keys to Successful Co-Parenting* (Perigee).

Mel Krantzler's *Creative Divorce* (Adams Media Corporation) and *Divorcing* (St. Martins), the latter co-authored with Melvin Belli, are more descriptive in nature, telling the reader what to expect. In *Divorcing*, the goal seems to be a comprehensive guide. Krantzler's books describe rather than suggest much. There is a bias toward getting back into a relationship as a main healing strategy.

Although there is not a lot of what-to-do in the book, *Second Chances: Men, Women, and Children a Decade After Divorce* (Houghton Mifflin) gives you some ideas about what each family member is going to experience. The authors are Judith S. Wallerstein and Sandra Blakeslee.

On a humorous note there are three titles that are the funny version of the recovery books: Elizabeth Kuster's *Exorcising Your Ex* (Fireside) and Cynthia Heimel's *Get Your Tongue Out Of My Mouth, I'm Kissing You Goodbye* (Fawcett Books) and *If You Can't Live Without Me, Why Aren't You Dead Yet?* (Harperperennial Library) It's great that we have these books.

APPENDIX C:
Other Publications
by Pat Hudson

BOOKS

Making Friends with Your Unconscious Mind: The User Friendly Guide (The Center Press): 1993.
The Solution-Oriented Woman: Creating the Life You Want (W. W. Norton): 1986.

Coauthored

Rewriting Love Stories: Brief Marital Therapy (Norton Professional Books): 1991.
Stop Blaming, Start Loving: A Solution-Oriented Approach to Improving Your Relationship (W. W. Norton): 1995.

AUDIOTAPES

All of my audiotapes are self published.
Self-Hypnosis, Volume I: Pain Control and Health
Self-Hypnosis, Volume II: Smoking Cessation

Other Publications by Pat Hudson

Self Hypnosis, Volume III: Academic Performance
Find Yourself in Your Dreams
Leave Your Divorce in the Dust
What It Really Takes to Stay Married

INDEX

Index

Index

Index